Do Fish
Know
They're
WET?

Do Fish Know They're WET?

Living in Your World—
Without Getting Hooked

TOM NEVEN

BakerBooks
Grand Rapids, Michigan

Published by Baker Books
a division of Baker Publishing Group
P.O. Box 6287, Grand Rapids, MI 49516-6287
www.bakerbooks.com

Third printing, October 2005

Printed in the United States of America

Library of Congress Cataloging-in-Publication Data
Neven, Tom, 1956–
    Do fish know they're wet? : living in your world—without getting hooked / Tom Neven.
       p.   cm.
    Includes bibliographical references.
    ISBN 0-8010-6518-6 (pbk.)
    1. Christianity—Philosophy. 2. Christianity and culture. 3. Christian life.
I. Title.
BR100.N39 2005
230—dc22   2004021442

To my wife, Colette, and to my children, Joshua and Hannah, who showed great patience as I spent so much time on the computer writing this book.

Also to Dr. Arthur Holmes and Dr. David Fletcher for instilling in me a love of ideas and an understanding of their consequences.

Contents

Introduction

~~~~~~~~~~~~~~~~~~~~

Why Is a Worldview Important?

Back when my parents were young, they had an expression for a person who was mistaken about something. They'd say, "He's all wet!" As I grew up, my parents frequently reminded me that I was all wet. Hey, that was their job.

Thinking about the many times I was told this reminds me of a nice Japanese rock garden I once visited. It had a beautiful pond filled with giant goldfish and koi. When people threw little bits of food in the water, the fish would fight and squirm over the treat, sometimes to the point that some fish were completely out of the water, wriggling across the backs of their buddies. I wondered if they could feel they were in air and not water, just as we feel when we're in water and not air, especially if we didn't intend to be there. There's nothing like being thrown fully clothed into a pool to make you realize that you're a land creature. Being on dry land is natural, something we don't think about. Water is not our natural environment.

But have you ever thought you might be immersed in an environment and not know it? You could be all wet and not realize it because it feels natural.

That environment is today's postmodern, post-Christian culture. (I'll explain these terms in more detail later.) Most of the world is all wet when it comes to understanding truth. But we're not supposed to be like the world. In other words, if the world is all wet, we should feel uncomfortable in it. But how many Christians are truly uncomfortable in this environment?

Sure, we're careful to stay away from the usual suspects like trashy TV and raunchy movies. Hardcore gangsta rap is off-limits, as is violent thrash metal. Racy magazine ads are verboten. But it goes much deeper than that. For example, do you believe that if something is legal, then it's right? Do you believe that at heart all religions are true? Do you believe that there are no absolutes? Are you absolutely sure?

If you're not sure of your answers to some of these questions (and many others in this book), you may be all wet. Why does it matter what you think about law, literature, or politics? Why does your worldview matter?

Your worldview matters because it affects the way you live your Christian life, share the gospel, and become a good citizen, parent, or friend. Basically, a worldview is the lens through which you see everything. Maybe you've heard the expression that a person sees the world through rose-colored glasses. This means everything he sees is rosy, whether or not it really is. This person might not even realize he has these glasses on. As you can imagine, this could be dangerous. Have you considered that maybe you're looking at everything through world-colored glasses instead of Christ-colored ones?

Ask yourself if you really believe that what you believe is really real. Not what you say, but what you believe in your heart. What you *really* believe is your worldview.

Get Real!

The basic concept that drives your worldview is what you think about the nature of reality. Not everyone sees reality the same way. Some people don't even believe in reality.

I once was having coffee with a group of people who believed the world was really just a big illusion—this, while they were drinking out of very real coffee cups, sitting on very real chairs at a very real table. I asked them, "Do you look both ways before crossing the street?"

"Y-y-y-esss . . ." one answered tentatively, wondering what that had to do with the nature of reality.

"Well," I answered, "that oncoming bus is either real or it's not. Do you step in front of it because you're sure it's just an illusion?"

In other words, people live with certain rules, certain presuppositions, whether or not they realize it. That's the way God made us. It's easy to speculate about reality and illusions when we have no personal stake in the answer. But in our hearts we don't really believe what we're claiming, even if we're not fully conscious of that.

This is part of what I call the "Munsters Principle." You may have seen reruns of this 1960s TV show about a family of lovable monsters: Herman, the Frankenstein-like dad; Lily, the vampirish mom; Eddie, the wolfman-like son; and Grandpa, another vampire. Only Marilyn, the teenage niece, was "normal."

But wait! What's normal? While *The Munsters* attempted to be funny—emphasis on the word *attempted*—by turning upside down concepts like good and bad or ugly and beautiful, the show missed the larger point. You must already have a concept of good to recognize bad. You must already have some understanding of beauty to distinguish ugliness. This is the way we're hardwired. Think about what the apostle Paul had to say: "Finally, brothers, whatever is true, whatever is noble, whatever is right, whatever is pure, whatever is lovely, whatever is admirable—if anything is excellent or praiseworthy—think about such things" (Phil. 4:8). He is assuming we already have a concept of "true," "noble," and so forth.

11

Our culture recently received a shock that forced us to re-evaluate such matters. David S. Dockery wrote, "The events of September 11, 2001, shook the moral ground of Western civilization. A major blow was struck against the sweeping tides of moral relativism. Discussions of good and bad, right and wrong, which had degenerated merely to what is 'good or bad for you,' or more likely to what is 'functional' or 'dysfunctional,' were changed. As our society stared evil in the face on that day, questions regarding moral absolutes again entered the public square."[1]

But, you might say, didn't the terrorists claim they were doing a good thing by following the will of Allah? That proves my point. Notice they didn't say they were doing an evil thing. No, they tried to justify their actions by putting them within the framework of good and righteousness. Even in their hearts they knew that people shouldn't do evil things; they just chose to redefine good and evil, perhaps on a subconscious level. Paul wrote, "When Gentiles, who do not have the law [that was given to the Jews], do by nature things required by the law, they are a law for themselves, even though they do not have the law, since they show that the requirements of the law are written on their hearts, their consciences also bearing witness, and their thoughts now accusing, now even defending them" (Rom. 2:14–15).

C. S. Lewis noted that there has never been a culture that celebrated cowardice or rewarded treachery. Of course, history is full of cowards and betrayal, but again, people choose to call it something else, knowing deep in their hearts that such things are bad.

Just as there is a physical reality, there are also moral and spiritual realities, even if some people don't recognize them or choose to deny them—at least until a violation of such realities hurts them, kind of like the spiritual or moral equivalent of an oncoming bus. That's the nature of things as God created them. And violating any one of these realities inevitably proves another. If you're playing around on the roof of your house, ignoring the rule of prudence, you'll soon be obeying the law of gravity.

So, keep these ideas in mind as we proceed through this book. We're going to go to the basic nature of things, things that might not have occurred to you even though you've been living by them all along.

Let's start by laying down a few basic rules:

Rule No. 1: *God is.* It's as simple as that. Either God exists or he doesn't. He is the ultimate reality.

Rule No. 2: *God is the God of truth. All truth is God's truth.*

Rule No. 3: *Because we are created in God's image, we have the ability to recognize truth, although that ability is tainted by sin.*

Rule No. 4: *The ability of a person to recognize truth diminishes the closer that truth is to his or her own heart, to the very nature of being a person.* (This takes a little thinking about, but it will become clearer as we go.)

Rule No. 5: *Christianity is dangerous to the world system.* The "world" recognizes this, even if only unconsciously. That's why you can talk about God, Buddha, Krishna, or Allah all you want and no one really gets upset, but once you mention the name Jesus Christ, the reaction is fierce. Jesus said the world will hate Christians because it hates him (John 15:18–21). People hate Jesus because his very name convicts them of their sin even if they can't fully articulate that.

That said, here are a few ideas to reject:

No. 1: *There are no absolutes.*

No. 2: *Everything is relative; truth depends on the situation.*

The Big Picture

To develop a Christian worldview, we need to be able to step back, to try to see the whole picture. We must be able to see reality as a sort of structure, a *truth structure* that upholds everything else. We must also realize that our culture sometimes makes it hard to see this structure.

Unfortunately, too many Christians put different parts of their lives in little boxes. This part of my life is faith; this part is work;

this part is entertainment. But if God is the God of all truth, then everything is connected. I hope as you read this book you'll see the interconnectedness of many issues facing us today. Issues in science affect politics. Problems in politics affect our view of humankind. Changes in the use of language lead to horrific acts.

This book will not provide automatic answers to all questions. I hope you'll be challenged to think Christianly about certain issues. In doing so, you'll find that answers to certain questions will come naturally or—I can't deny this—not so naturally. The point is, I hope that you'll at least know the right questions to ask.

With that, let's get started.

1

How We Got Here

If you like history, as I do, you might see our past as a series of "chunks," eras of different lengths that can be grouped together. For example, the period from AD 33 to about AD 500 might be called the church fathers chunk. The years AD 500 to about AD 1100 might be the medieval chunk. Of course, it's not quite that neat and distinct, and the transitions between chunks might be a bit blurry, but I find this method helpful for visualizing history.

Having said that, it's hard to know at which chunk to begin when discussing how we got from there to here, since every chunk influenced the ones that came after. But I think it's a safe bet to begin our journey at the Enlightenment, that period of time from the late 1600s to late 1700s when people began to rely more on rational inquiry than religious faith in determining truth. (The Enlightenment, for that matter, couldn't have happened without the Renaissance and the Reformation, but you have to start somewhere.) There's nothing wrong with rational inquiry; God gave us minds and the ability to reason. It's when people started to get a bit cocky, thinking they could figure out everything, from how the earth orbited the sun to how to determine right and wrong, that we started to get into trouble.

Even the term *Enlightenment* carries the sense that human minds had been dark before and these thinkers had come along to turn on the lights. The overall worldview that resulted from the Enlightenment was modernism, a philosophy that in many ways is still present today.

Many great discoveries happened during this time. The Enlightenment helped kick off the Industrial Revolution, a time when new machinery was developed that greatly improved life.

During this time people also began to use rational inquiry to draw conclusions about life. Rational inquiry is particularly useful for one branch of knowledge—science. People began to think that unless something could be seen, felt, tasted, smelled, or heard, it didn't exist. If it couldn't be tested, it wasn't real. This was a form of knowledge called empiricism.

You might see where this is heading. To call something "wrong" or "right" was not something that could be tested or sensed. It wasn't a very large leap to say that if right and wrong were not empirically verifiable, they must be nothing better than opinion. The same thinking was applied to truth, beauty, and any number of ideas that people couldn't really put their hands on, so to speak. Enlightenment thinkers were rational skeptics—prove it to us or we won't believe it.

THE DARK AGES

You sometimes might hear the term *Dark Ages* used in place of *medieval*, which was meant to be a deliberate insult to that time before the Enlightenment. In fact, one dictionary gives one meaning of medieval as "old-fashioned, especially lacking modern enlightened attitudes."

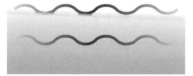

16

Revealed truth in the form of religion, particularly Christianity, carried no weight with these thinkers, since it wasn't testable. Although many Enlightenment thinkers were Christians, particularly Isaac Newton and Johannes Kepler, some people called deists tried to compromise. They saw the universe as a machine or a billiards table. Cause A inevitably led to result B. Deists didn't want to do away with God, so they simply defined him as the Grand Watchmaker who had set the machine in motion and then left the scene. Their "god" was not personally involved in maintaining the universe, so he couldn't be involved in any individual's life. Still other Enlightenment thinkers were actively hostile to religion in general and Christianity in particular. The French philosopher Voltaire is the most notorious example.

At first life went along happily in this billiard-ball universe, but over time the rational approach to life seemed cold and impersonal, and some became dissatisfied with the modernist view. There had to be something better. In the late 1700s a group of people called romantics emerged. They weren't romantics in the sense of kisses and red roses, but in the sense that they saw the world in starkly different ways from the modernists. Instead of hard, cold rationality, they liked nature. They saw the mountains, forests, rivers—the natural world—as the highest good. It was a time when people were beginning to explore the wilder reaches of the North American continent, and the heroic explorer (à la Daniel Boone and Davy Crockett) was an ideal. American Indians came to be seen as noble savages, a view seen most prominently in James Fenimore Cooper's *The Last of the Mohicans.* An art movement called the Hudson River school of painting arose about this time, characterized by beautiful images of wild rivers, mountains, and forests but noticeably lacking the blizzards, pestilence, and other potentially dangerous aspects of nature.

With the rise of romanticism, personified by men such as French philosopher Jean-Jacques Rousseau, came a subtle change in the view of human nature. No longer were people beings who were created by God, had fallen into sin, and needed a redeemer. People, the romantics said, were basically good, and it was society, cold

17

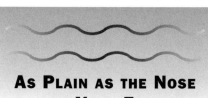

AS PLAIN AS THE NOSE ON YOUR FACE

God's Word in the Bible is revealed truth. But the Bible also says there are some things that should be obvious to anyone, which is not revealed truth. Another way to look at these things is to call them *special revelation* and *general revelation*.

An example of special revelation is Jesus's statement in John 14:6: "I am the way and the truth and the life. No one comes to the Father except through me." This is not something you can learn from looking at the world around you.

An example of general revelation is Paul's statement in Romans 1:19, where he asserts that no one can say God does not exist because God has made his existence plain to them.

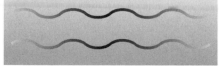

and mechanized, that corrupted them. This missed the obvious question, of course: If people are inherently good, how did society become corrupted?

Both the modernist worldview and the romantic worldview bubbled along during most of the 1800s, but modernism seemed to be winning out, especially after the Civil War showed that "basically good" people were willing to kill each other in truly horrifying numbers. Several decades of exploring the West proved that nature was not always kind. It was hard to see Native Americans as noble savages as they massacred wagon trains full of settlers. Heroic explorers were no better, massacring villages full of natives.

The rational skeptics of the Enlightenment began to see life as futile. The promises of modernism hadn't come true. Science and rationality had not made the world a better place; in fact, they had merely led to better, more efficient ways for people to slaughter each other. World War I and then the Russian Revolution in 1917 greatly diminished the optimism of modernism.

Out of this disillusionment came postmodernism. Modernism couldn't answer the ultimate questions of life—what is good, what is true, what is noble. If modernism couldn't answer these questions, people reasoned, there must not be any answers.

Thus postmodernists contend that truth doesn't exist. Concepts such as beauty, nobility, truth, and goodness are nothing more than social constructs or stories that a society creates to explain itself. These stories, or narratives, are pulled together under a metanarrative—a grand story, so to speak. But that's all it is—a story. No society, no religion, no belief system is better than any other. In fact, if you say your way is better than another, you are guilty of intolerance. This, of course, creates problems for Christians who take seriously Christ's declaration that he is *the* way, *the* truth, *the* life.

When there is no truth, all that remains is power. That is why our political system has become so distorted in recent decades. Politics has always been a rough-and-tumble business, but it has become nastier lately. In many ways we have lost the things that bind together people from every continent and culture into one society called the United States of America: an agreement, more or less, about the answers to the big questions. If we can't agree on such things, all that's left is for one side to impose its will on the other.

You can see where this can lead. Under the postmodernist view, rights are just a social construct. Rights are something the government grants us, not something we have because, in the words of the Declaration of Independence, we are all created equal by God, and these rights cannot be taken away by anyone, government included. You'll hear a lot of talk about rights in current political debates, but if postmodernism is true—there's a real oxymoron—then the concept of "rights" is just someone's opinion. In fact, one moral philosophy that grew in the last century was utilitarianism, which declares something good if it brings the greatest good to the greatest number of people. Under such a system, the concept of rights means nothing, since if killing me brings greater good to the larger group, I have no right to object.

19

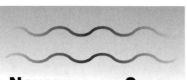

NONSENSE ON STILTS

The utilitarian philosopher Jeremy Bentham called the concept of rights "nonsense on stilts." Ironically, Bentham was a strong abolitionist, but his stand against slavery wasn't because the human rights of slaves were being violated. It was because, in the utilitarian calculation, it was not a useful system that brought the greatest good to the greatest number. You wonder how he did the math.

Today we live with a bizarre hybrid of modernism and postmodernism. We have people appealing to the rigors of science while a book on New Age shamanism rests on their bedside stand. The wonders of space exploration or genetic science coexist with witchcraft. In a modernist culture, New Age religion should be laughed off the stage (and some people do that), but it is tolerated because it is no threat to the overarching system. But Christianity, a faith rooted in history and facts, is not tolerated because it makes claims that go against both modernism and postmodernism. It is Rule No. 5 kicking in.

Keep this brief history lesson in mind as we proceed through this book. Modernism and postmodernism color every aspect of your life, but you can develop a coherent Christian worldview.

2

In the Know

Bob: There's a cat under the table.
Sally: How do you know?
Bob: Because I see it.
Sally: But do you really see it?
Bob: I know it's there because I hear it meowing.
Sally: But do you really hear it?
Bob: What are you talking about?
Sally: Can you ever really *know* anything? Do you really *know* there's a cat under the table? Do you even know there's a table?

Now there's a conversation that's going nowhere fast. Is Sally just giving Bob a hard time? Perhaps, but several famous philosophers have made a name for themselves by questioning what is real. How can we know what we know? What is the difference between *knowledge* and *belief*?

There's a whole realm of philosophy called *epistemology*—the study of knowledge. It's a pretty technical field, but for simplicity's

21

sake, I'm going to put it in terms of baseball. Three umpires are talking together. The first umpire says, "There are balls and strikes, and I call 'em as I see 'em."

The second umpire says, "No, there are balls and strikes, and I call 'em as they are."

The third umpire says, "There are balls and strikes, and they're nothing until I say what they are."

That pretty well summarizes what epistemology tries to get at. Does something exist because we perceive it? Do we perceive it because it is? Or do we define reality the way we want to?

What Can We Truly Know?

For many centuries people just knew what they knew—or at least what they thought they knew. Nobody really thought about knowing. But early in the Enlightenment period, when people were starting to rely on rational inquiry more than faith, the philosopher René Descartes wanted to prove that *something* existed. (It's the most basic question of philosophy: Why is there something rather than nothing?) He realized that much of what people thought they "knew" could be doubted. Everyone knew there was a God, but Descartes said that if you think seriously about it, you can doubt there's a God. He narrowed his search, finding more and more things he could doubt until he was faced with the final question: Do I exist?

As he continued to doubt, he realized that something or someone was doubting—that is, thinking. That was the most basic unit of knowledge. There was a thing that was thinking. That's where he hit on the proof of his existence: "I think, therefore I am."

Basic to this philosophy is the idea that we have fixed ideas in our minds that then correspond to things we see. We have the idea of a leaf and recognize it on a tree, and so forth.

Seems pretty obvious, but what Descartes did was to separate knowledge from faith. It put the thinking human first, not the fact of his being—and by default, the being of God, although Descartes did not intend that. We moved from *being* to *knowing*. It started with rational thinking, not previous knowledge. The wisdom of the ages was doubtable. Descartes's rationalism was a great boon to science, but in philosophy it would prove disastrous; it's possible to draw a straight line from Descartes to today's postmodernism and existentialism.

The Blank Slate

John Locke, whose thinking had a great effect on our nation's founding fathers, started with the opposite premise from Descartes. He said we do not have any natural preconceptions of leaves, trees, or anything. Our mind at birth was a tabula rasa, a blank slate. What we know as adults comes only through the experiences that

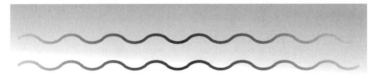

GET REAL!

In a way, Descartes's idea that people have preconceived notions of things was much like that of the Greek philosopher Plato, who said people have ideas of a perfect tree but never encounter one in the material world; it exists only in the perfect world of "forms." That's why the Greeks came to consider the physical, material world corrupt and evil—something to be avoided. This is contrary to Christianity, which teaches that God created the material world and declared it good.

"write" knowledge on that slate. But we might perceive things incorrectly. A person at a distance may look to be a man but is really a woman. An oar in the water looks bent, even though we know it's perfectly straight. According to Locke, anything that can't be sensed doesn't exist. Without ears, there is no such thing as sound. So, if a tree fell in the forest and no one was there to hear it, it didn't fall. (It didn't even exist.)

But How Do You *Know*?

The Scottish philosopher David Hume was like Locke in that he believed we could know nothing without first perceiving it. And he took Descartes's doubting to its logical extreme. We can be skeptical about everything, even the thoughts that the "I" is supposedly thinking. He said Descartes's idea of a "self" could not be known outside of perceiving it. It was, in a way, an idea without proof in the real world. The implications are that we can never truly know anything. We might have good reason to act in a certain way—the bridge hasn't fallen down in all the times I've crossed it, so it must be safe today—but we can never be sure. Accordingly, what we believe to be true about the moral realm, even the existence of God, could not be known for sure.

Immanuel Kant tried to answer Hume, but on a strictly rational basis, he couldn't. Without meaning to, however, Kant reinforced the idea that God cannot truly be known, since the rational mind could not reach that conclusion. Believing in God was a leap of faith.

The Road to Postmodernism

As the nineteenth century progressed, the culture started to become disenchanted with the modernism of the Enlightenment. Not only was the universe a cold, impersonal place, but it apparently had no God, since science couldn't prove there was a thing called God. Any lingering optimism of the Enlightenment was

24

dealt its deathblow by Friedrich Nietzsche. Since we couldn't know that we existed, did our lives have any meaning? Is human reason capable of knowing anything? This, in the end, was a form of *nihilism*—the belief that life is pointless and that there is no objective basis for truth, beauty, and the like. (*Nihil* is the Latin word for "nothing.") It is a destructive philosophy that touches much of modern life in one way or another.

Nietzsche was ahead of his time, but by the mid-twenthieth century, existentialists such as Albert Camus and Jean-Paul Sartre took Nietzsche to his logical conclusion: any knowledge of reality is beyond us. All we know is ourselves, so at least we can tell stories, or narratives, about ourselves. The stories that a culture tells itself become a *metanarrative*—an overarching story, but still just a story.

So, if all that's left is competing stories, none of which can be known to be true, all that's left is power. Your metanarrative simply masks an attempt to lord power over everyone else.

Even the very nature of what it means to be human comes into doubt. We are who we are by the language we use to talk about ourselves. Nietzsche said the only authentic life was that of the *Übermensch*, sometimes translated as "Superman" but better rendered as "Overman"—the man who by force of his will rises above the herd. (Hitler touted this ideology when he rose to power about forty years later.) The existentialism of Sartre plays off this as well. He said that existence precedes essence—in other words, we exist before we define who we are. Our inner being, our essence, is therefore whatever we make of it. There is no core human nature.

The Way Out

As you will see in this book, postmodernism has infected every corner of our culture—even the church. Taken seriously, postmodernism means the death of ethics, the death of history, the death of truth itself.

But there is a way out. The chief mistake of people like Descartes, Hume, and Nietzsche is that they assume there is only one way of knowing—through our mind. But we are both physical and spiritual beings. We can know things through our physical senses, of course, but we can know things in our spirit too. An unbelieving world knows in its spirit that something is wrong. We have a hole in us, although we don't know what it is, how it was caused, or how to fix it. This is not something perceived through the senses, although its playing out is obvious: war, hatred, theft, lying, malice—on and on.

As redeemed believers, we can know spiritual things directly. "The Spirit himself testifies with our spirit that we are God's children" (Rom. 8:16). The Bible talks about knowledge on a deep, spiritual level, an intimacy the fallen world cannot know. And this is the difference between knowledge of the head and knowledge of the heart. Matthew 7:22–23 contains a frightening idea—many people know God in a head-knowledge way, but they never know him spiritually. Jesus said, "Many will say to me on that day, 'Lord, Lord, did we not prophesy in your name, and in your name drive out demons and perform many miracles?' Then I will tell them plainly, 'I never knew you. Away from me, you evildoers!'"

The word *know* here, as used throughout the Bible, is that deep, spiritual knowledge. It's sometimes used to describe sexual relations—Adam *knew* Eve—because that's what the marriage relationship is supposed to be like: head knowledge, of course, but also knowing one another on a deep spiritual level. That's the way we should know God.

3

Behold, Man!

Here's a great Yiddish word: *mensch*. It literally means "man," but this word carries a lot of freight. It means a man of integrity, honor, courage, and every other good quality you could think of. A man's man! It's the highest compliment to say of someone, "He's a real mensch!"

Notice that we never say such a thing about animals. "Well, I'll tell ya, Bob, he was a real cat's cat!" Why do we never speak of superlative cats, crows, or caribou? In fact, we never say, "He was a bad cat." We can say he was big, ugly, or destructive, but we never make moral judgments of animals. (If a cat couldn't catch mice, climb trees, or be generally smug, we could say it was a bad cat in a factual sense, but not in a moral sense.) In fact, when we say someone is behaving like an animal—meaning he's doing something immoral—we're being unfair to the animals!

Most people instinctively seem to make a distinction between people and animals. Why? What is it about humans that puts them into a category all by themselves?

27

I'll answer that a bit later, because, well, some people don't think that's the case. Back in the 1960s, anthropologist Desmond Morris wrote *The Naked Ape*, which pretty much pioneered the field of evolutionary anthropology. He made explicit what had only been assumed—that because we share some characteristics with animals, mainly primates, we must therefore be nothing more than animals ourselves.

It didn't take too long for that thinking to permeate the culture. For example, Ingrid Newkirk of the People for the Ethical Treatment of Animals (PETA) once said, "A rat is a pig is a dog is a boy." Others say no animal should ever be harmed in research that might benefit human lives; in other words, we won't harm rats to test a medicine that might save thousands of human lives.

How could animal rights activists arrive at such an opinion? Two hundred years ago such thinking would have been unthinkable. What happened in the meantime?

Charles Darwin, that's what.

While I'll deal more with science and specifically evolution in chapter 13, what we need to know now is that Darwin's *Origin of Species*, the book that first introduced his theories, shook up more than the scientific world. A worldview called scientific naturalism (sometimes called scientific materialism), which was born during the Enlightenment, became a prominent worldview in Western culture and colored our outlook on many topics outside of science.

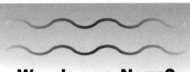

WHAT'S IN A NAME?

Throughout this book I'll use the noun *man* and pronouns *he/his/him* when speaking of humankind. I'm not leaving women out of the equation. Rather, I'm basing this on the English language, which has historically used *man* generically and has no generic third-person singular pronoun. In English, *man* serves as the gender-neutral term for humankind.

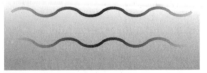

According to scientific naturalism, all that exists is matter and energy; there is no supernatural realm, no God, no spirit. We're all just the product of colliding atoms, stray molecules, and random chance. Perhaps no one made this point better than the late Carl Sagan, the astronomer made famous by his TV documentary *Cosmos*. In the opening episode of that series, Sagan, sitting amid the glory of nature, confidently asserts, "The cosmos is all that is, or ever was, or ever will be." Poof—just like that, Sagan attempted to make God disappear, and because Sagan was an intelligent scientist, most viewers simply accepted his statement as true.

So what does this have to do with a Christian view of man? Well, the nonscientific outworking of thinking such as Sagan's is secular humanism. Now, a lot of stuff gets blamed on secular humanism, some of which doesn't fit the label. That's not to say, however, that such a movement does not exist. There's a publication called *The Humanist*, then there's "A Humanist Manifesto" (a sort of foundational document for humanists), and the Humanist Society.

A strong proponent of secular humanism was Sir Julian Huxley. He was the grandson of Thomas Huxley, who was called "Darwin's Bulldog" for the ferociousness with which he defended Darwin's views. Julian Huxley pretty much defined the way humanists looked at man: "I use the word 'Humanist' to mean someone who believes that man is just as much a natural phenomenon as an animal or a plant, that his body, his mind, and his soul were not supernaturally created but are all products of evolution, and that he is not under the control or guidance of any supernatural Being or beings, but has to rely on himself and his own powers."[1]

Pretty much pushes God out of the picture, no? But ironically, Huxley still could not get God out of his thinking. In an essay called "The New Divinity," he wrote, "Man emerged as the dominant type on earth about a million years ago, but has only been really effective as a psychosocial organism for under ten thousand years. In that mere second of cosmic time, he has produced astonishing achievements—but has also been guilty of unprecedented horrors and follies."[2]

The horrors and follies part is without dispute. But judged against what? Remember what I said in the introduction? How can you have a concept of crooked without first understanding straight? If we're just bits and pieces that just happened to come together over millions of years, what is "horror" or "folly"? These are moral terms, not naturalistic ones. If he were intellectually honest, he would have said they were merely his opinions, but I suspect he didn't really see it that way. He had an innate sense of crooked and straight, which conformed to the biblical view of things but not the naturalistic one.

This creates problems for scientific naturalists, although many don't even see the difficulty. They work under assumptions that are really part of what it means to be created in God's image. If they really believe that what they believe is really real, they'll hide in their closets in stark terror, for the world would be a terrifying place. And it has great potential to be so.

Millions of Dead

Tens of millions of murders can be laid at the feet of Karl Marx, the founding father of communism. The young Marx was strongly influenced in the early 1800s by the German philosopher Georg Hegel, who taught that human history was in a constant state of forward motion—progress, in other words. One society existed until the internal contradictions led it to be replaced by another, better society, always moving forward toward greater freedom and perfection.

Marx kept Hegel's idea of progress, but it was expressed primarily in social relationships, which themselves were influenced by whatever economic class you happened to belong to: the proletariat (working class) or the bourgeois (those who owned most of the wealth and exploited the proletariat).

Marx believed that society molded men, not the other way around. In other words, if you wanted to improve mankind, you had to improve society first. You would then create what Marx called the "New Man." Of course, we're certainly influenced by the society we live in, but not at the fundamental, core level of what it means to be human. The society we live in might determine our taste in food and music or influence the way we interact with others. It does not determine our need for love, human contact, and all those other things at our core.

The Marxist ideal, then, is to change society first. And because Marxism, through Hegel, was imbued with the idea of historical inevitability, anything that stood in the way of Marxist ideals was against progress, against history itself. For that reason, all Marxist revolutions produced great horrors, including bloody affairs in Russia (1917), China (1949), and Cambodia (1975). To Marxists, people had no inherent worth. They were not beings created in God's image and of infinite worth; they were merely members of a class. (The next chapter explains the inevitable result of this.) For that reason, people could easily be eliminated if they got in the way of "progress."

That'll Make You Drool

If we are nothing more than animals, maybe there is some link between the way animals behave and the way we do. The Russian psychologist Ivan Pavlov was the first to make this assertion, founding a theory of human behavior called behavioralism. Basically, we are simply a product of our previous conditioning. Everything that we do now has been influenced by our earlier experiences.

Pavlov experimented with stimulus and response, training dogs to salivate simply at the sound of a bell, since through long conditioning they came to associate the bell with feeding time. (They'd salivate even if no food appeared.) Another later psychologist, B. F. Skinner, took this idea and used laboratory rats and mazes to make the same point.

Not too many people hold to strict behavioralism anymore, as studies have shown human behavior is affected by many factors, not just those experiences we've previously had.

Sometimes a Cigar Is Just a Cigar

Another view of human nature, still a form of behavioralism, has strongly influenced us today—Freudianism, founded by Sigmund Freud, a psychologist and the father of psychoanalysis. (Think of all those cartoons you've seen of a patient on a couch and a doctor smoking a cigar or pipe while taking notes.)

The human mind, according to Freud, consists of the id, the ego, and the superego. The id is the pleasure principle, those instinctual drives that make us seek immediate satisfaction. The ego is the conscious mind, serving as a sort of traffic cop between the real world and the id. Finally, the superego is that part of the mind that holds conscience, moral norms, and the like that we're taught by parents and society from earliest childhood. The ego is also caught in the conflict between the id and the superego. No wonder Freud thought we were all so screwed up! But all these things were really nothing more than physical brain states—things that came about through interaction of nerves, chemicals, the brain, and so forth.

Freud said the variety of mental illnesses were just products of the mind, the mental faculties of the person. For Freud, everything had a cause, even things we would classify as strictly mental. (There's the behavioralism element.) Things we would normally pay no mind to—sorry for the pun—could all be traced to some mental event. Slips of the tongue (Freudian slips), dreams and neuroses, and other matters could be tied to some hidden part of the person's mind. This is a form of determinism, meaning we really have no free will; everything is caused by something else, even if we're unaware of it. Even the superego is a product of someone else's teaching. (Freud never answered the question of who was the first person to teach these things some time way back in prehistory.)

Some things that were once conscious mental states can be repressed so that we are no longer aware of them—childhood sexual abuse, for example. Repressing events did not prevent them from affecting one's future actions, though. That explains Freud's preoccupation with unconscious mental states. According to his thinking,

32

there are all sorts of things going on in our minds that cause us to do what we do. It is the job of the psychoanalyst to dig up these states to get at why we did this or that. But this theory gives people a lot of excuses for their horrible behavior. "Oh, my mom must have locked me in a closet when I was a kid, so that's why I robbed the bank." Don't laugh. All sorts of deviant behaviors are now being excused or at least soft-pedaled based on this view of man.

I Gotta Be Me

Back in the first chapter I talked about the romantic movement that was a reaction to the Enlightenment. One of the major thinkers in romanticism was Jean-Jacques Rousseau, who said,

REFUSING TO SEE

Carl Rogers, writing in the *Journal of Humanistic Psychology*, said, "For myself, though I am well aware of the incredible amount of destructive, cruel, malevolent behavior in today's world—from the threats of war to the senseless violence in the streets—I do not find that this evil is inherent in human nature."[3]

He sees the symptoms but refuses to see the disease. He simply refuses to change a fundamental belief, even in the face of overwhelming evidence to the contrary.

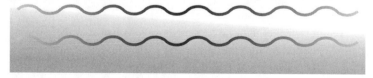

"If man is good by nature, as I believe to have shown him to be, it follows that he stays like that as long as nothing foreign to him corrupts him."

That thing "foreign to him" would be society or culture. But Rousseau missed an obvious question: how can society or culture become corrupt if men are basically good? There is no answer. There's a strong element of self-delusion or, worse yet, willful blindness that goes along with this idea.

But to follow Rousseau's thinking to its logical conclusion, if we're basically good, what should be our highest aim? Why, "self-actualization"—doing your own thing, basically. Be all you can be. An army of one.

Psychologist Abraham Maslow believed as Rousseau did. "Since the inner nature is good or neutral rather than bad, it is best to bring it out and to encourage it rather than to suppress it," he wrote. "If it is permitted to guide our life, we grow healthy, fruitful, and happy."[4]

Maslow is perhaps most famous for formulating the human's hierarchy of needs, with the highest need being self-actualization.

So, if I have natural urges to molest children, why shouldn't I? Maslow might be horrified at such a suggestion, but he wouldn't really have grounds to object. And this is precisely the argument homosexual activists use to justify their behavior; they were "born" gay, so why not live that way? In fact, an organization called the North American Man-Boy Love Association (NAMBLA) is using this argument to try to decriminalize pedophilia.

And as much as it might be painful to admit, they have a point— *if* man is nothing but atoms, impulses, and brain states. But that's where they get it wrong.

Angst

Another view of man arose shortly before World War II. It was called existentialism. Popularized by Jean-Paul Sartre and Albert Camus, the existentialists believed that the world had no mean-

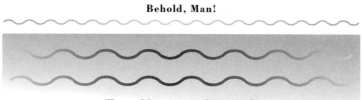

THE HUMAN STAIN?

As animal rights activists deny man's unique status in creation, radical environmentalists deny God's mandate for man to have dominion over creation. (These people are often one and the same.)

Such people believe nature is the highest thing, and anything that intrudes on nature is bad. Humans, then, are a stain upon nature. Activist protests take many forms: destroying homes and cars that pollute or are put where they "don't belong" to driving spikes into trees so that a logger's blade, upon hitting one, will shatter into many pieces, perhaps killing him. Better the tree live than the logger, apparently.

ing. In fact, Sartre said, "Existence precedes essence." By this, he meant that we exist without any meaning. There is no fixed essence of what it means to be human. We have to create our own meaning. We have to create our own rules. But for existentialists, everything in the end was meaningless. The world was absurd, and people who refused to see this were "inauthentic." (Does that term sound familiar?)

Existentialism is a dreary philosophy. Angst is its primary emotion—a feeling of dread that arises from our awareness of free choice. It is also an elitist philosophy. The inauthentic people were looked down upon as sheep.

35

After thinking through all the implications of existentialism, Camus came up with a diagnosis: the only logical thing to do was to commit suicide. Credit him at least with honesty.

In Our Creator's Image

So what is man? Genesis 1:26–28 says:

> Then God said, "Let us make man in our image, in our likeness, and let them rule over the fish of the sea and the birds of the air, over the livestock, over all the earth, and over all the creatures that move along the ground."
> So God created man in his own image, in the image of God he created him; male and female he created them.
> God blessed them and said to them, "Be fruitful and increase in number; fill the earth and subdue it. Rule over the fish of the sea and the birds of the air and over every living creature that moves on the ground."

So what does it mean to be created in God's image? Does this mean God has two eyes, a nose, and a mouth? No. John 4:24 clearly says that God is spirit. God has many attributes, some of which are "communicable" and others that aren't; in other words, God can pass some attributes on and others he can't. For example, his noncommunicable attributes include omniscience (knowing all things), omnipresence (being in all places at the same time), and omnipotence (having complete and universal power); these cannot belong to anyone other than God. But the communicable attributes can be passed on—for example, the ability to know and be known, the ability to give and receive love, a sense of right and wrong, and the desire to create.

The Great Explanation

The worldview that best explains reality as we experience it happens to be the Christian one. It can account for human behavior,

36

the presence of evil, how we got here, and many other questions
men have been asking over the centuries. Basically, it says we
were created good by God—but with a free will. He created us to
have fellowship with him, to love, obey, and worship him. But none
of these things can be forced; a robot can obey you, but it cannot
love you. Therefore, if we were to be able to truly love, obey, and
worship God, we had to have the ability *not* to.

Guess which one we chose.

That disobedience by the first people, Adam and Eve, called
the fall, has had terrible and lasting consequences. The doctrine
of original sin means that the penalty for the disobedience of our
first parents has been transmitted to every person ever conceived
(except for Jesus Christ, because he was conceived through the
Holy Spirit). King David wrote, "Surely I was sinful at birth, sinful
from the time my mother conceived me" (Ps. 51:5). And anyone
who doubts the idea of original sin need only look back on four
thousand years of recorded history for evidence.

We suffer from what theologians call "total depravity." Now
this doesn't mean we are as depraved as it's possible to be. Even
Jesus acknowledged that sinful men still know how to do good
things. He said, "Which of you, if his son asks for bread, will
give him a stone? Or if he asks for a fish, will give him a snake?
If you, then, though you are evil, know how to give good gifts to
your children, how much more will your Father in heaven give
good gifts to those who ask him!" (Matt. 7:9–11). Total depravity
means, rather, that sin has affected us in our totality; there's no
corner of our being that has not been touched by sin. That has
several bad results:

1. *God and man have become alienated.* Because of this alien-
   ation, no man truly seeks after God (Rom. 3:11). Instead, we
   create our own less-threatening gods, be they stone carv-
   ings, money, cars, music, booze or drugs, our jobs, or—very
   frequently—ourselves (Rom. 1:23). But still we sense that
   something is wrong. This accounts for all the religions in
   the world. Saint Augustine put his finger on the problem:

HUMAN DISTINCTIVES

What makes humans distinct from the animals? Some have said it's man's ability to make and use tools. But some animals do that too. Chimpanzees use sticks to get ants out of anthills, and one kind of bird uses twigs to draw nectar from flowers. What about language? It's pretty clear that many animals communicate to their own kind, and some—whales, porpoises, and other mammals—seem to have a fairly sophisticated system of communication.

What's left? Mark Twain said, "Man is the only animal that blushes—or needs to." He meant it as a derogatory joke toward the moralists of his day, but he's right. Only man has the ability to be ashamed or embarrassed. It goes all the way back to Genesis 3:7: "Then the eyes of both of them [Adam and Eve] were opened [after they sinned], and they realized they were naked; so they sewed fig leaves together and made coverings for themselves."

The German philosopher Arthur Schopenhauer said, "Man is the only animal who causes pain to others with no other object than wanting to do so." He's right too. Again, it goes back to the fall in Genesis. C. S. Lewis said that those who have the ability to be the best by necessity also have the ability to be the worst, and the Bible says we were created only a little lower than the angels—but then fell. We were created with the ability to show great compassion, but that

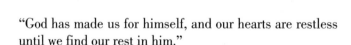

ability is corrupted by sin so that we now are also capable
of great malice.

But here's something else that sets man apart: our ability
to laugh. You'll never see a cat or dog laugh. (This is not
the same as playing.) The ability to laugh depends on us
understanding the world behaving in certain ways,
something only beings created in God's image can do.
When the twist of a joke upsets that expectation, we
laugh.

"God has made us for himself, and our hearts are restless
until we find our rest in him."

2. *Men are in conflict with each other.* All sorts of wars, murders,
fights, and arguments have blotted history (Matt. 24:6).

3. *Man is damaged within, both physically and spiritually.* Since
the fall, man has literally disintegrated. By this I mean that
the integration of body and spirit has come apart—we're
*dis*integrated. We suffer all sorts of mental and spiritual ailments, and anyone who's had anything from a cold to cancer
can attest to our damaged bodies (Gen. 2:17). Our spirits
are damaged too, and this results in physical problems. Dr.
S. I. McMillen, in his book *None of These Diseases*, notes
that emotions such as fear, sorrow, envy, or hatred can cause
actual physical ailments.

4. *Instead of being a steward over the creation, man's relationship with nature is now hostile and perverted.* Look at the
trash that lines roadsides. Look at a hill stripped bare of
trees, or a mountainside blown away for the precious ele-

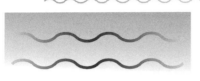

SHOWING OFF

The writer G. K. Chesterton described *paradox* as truth standing on its head to get attention. The Christian faith has many paradoxes: God becoming man; redeemed men who still sin; a kingdom already here but not yet completed.

ments it holds. Look at the garbage floating ashore at the beach or the smog covering most major cities. Need more evidence?

Of course, Christianity teaches that Jesus Christ died to pay the penalty for our sins, and he has already begun the process of redeeming both his people and the world. We live in the paradox of now but not yet. We're redeemed from our sins but still bear the mark of Adam—sin. The creation groans for its redemption (Rom. 8:23; 2 Cor. 5:2).

The gulf between God and man has been bridged. The apostle Paul wrote, "Once you were alienated from God and were enemies in your minds because of your evil behavior. But now he has reconciled you by Christ's physical body through death to present you holy in his sight, without blemish and free from accusation" (Col. 1:21–22).

The fact that Jesus was willing to pay the ultimate penalty for us shows that each and every person is infinitely precious in his sight. We are not just blobs of chemicals without purpose.

4

Neither Greek nor Jew . . .

Red and yellow, black and white,
They are precious in his sight,
Jesus loves the little children of the world.

Many of us grew up learning this song. No doubt the emphasis was on Jesus' love for everyone, but there's truth in its portrayal of the incredible diversity of people out there. Spend any time in a major city's airport and you'll see all the colors mentioned in the song—and more. You'll also see a lot of different cultures.

One of the major problems facing our world today is tribalism. It can be literally tribe against tribe, as in the massacre between the Tutsi and Hutu tribes in Rwanda in 1994. It can be excessive nationalism, racism, religious division, or gang warfare. Many

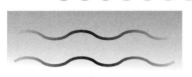

BET YOU DIDN'T KNOW

The word *barbarian* comes from the ancient Greeks, who considered all outsiders uncivilized and uncouth and mocked them by imitating what they thought their language sounded like: *bar, bar, bar.*

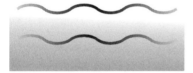

people find a way to lump themselves into a group and label everyone else as somehow inferior.

Such attitudes are found even in the Bible. In Numbers 12, Moses' brother and sister, Aaron and Miriam, began to complain that Moses had married a Cushite—that is, a dark-skinned woman. (Cush was what today we would call most of Ethiopia and Sudan.) Granted, their problem was more with Moses bossing them around than with his wife. Still, their stiff-necked attitude came out in the way they looked at the woman.

Only Skin Deep

Racism is a blot on mankind. To judge each other on such superficial characteristics as skin color, the width of one's nose, or the type of one's hair must grieve God. It is the literal definition of superficial.

Unfortunately, some seem to find a reason for racism in the Bible. Many slaveholders in the South before the Civil War cited Scripture as a justification for holding slaves, never mind that they took those passages out of their historical context, and the slavery practiced at that time bore little resemblance to that in the Bible.

There's still a crazy theory that God cursed black people because in the Genesis account of the sons of Noah, Noah did not bless Ham as he did the other sons, Shem and Japheth. And as Ham was the father of Cush, and Cush is the black part of Africa, some people assume black-skinned people are cursed. It's a real stretch, but then that has never stopped people from using God to justify their own hatred.

There's another crazy faction called British Israelism, sometimes called the Christian Identity Movement. According to these folks, the white people of northern Europe are descended from the lost tribes of Israel, and Jesus really came from these tribes; he was not a Jew from the tribe of Judah. They seem to forget that the lost tribes became "lost" because of disobedience to God; they were conquered and absorbed by the surrounding nations. These folks also have to throw out an awful lot of Old Testament prophecy to maintain their view.

Here should be our attitude: "There is neither Jew nor Greek, slave nor free, male nor female, for you are all one in Christ Jesus" (Gal. 3:28). The apostle Paul is throwing a wide net here, capturing every possible classification of people. To the early church, you were either Jewish or Greek, that is, a Gentile. You were either a slave or a free man. The male-female thing is fairly self-explanatory.

In other words, Paul is saying that all are equal in the sight of God—no ifs, ands, or buts.

Melting Pot or Tossed Salad?

In reaction to such division among people, a movement has arisen that attempts to unite races and cultures. Unfortunately, this movement ends up dividing more than uniting. More important, its underlying worldview is profoundly anti-Christian, being more informed by the Marxist view of man that I discussed in the previous chapter.

This movement disguises itself behind pleasant-sounding words that few people could object to—*multiculturalism, tolerance,* and *diversity*—assuming these people really mean what they say. And there's the problem: the people in this movement don't really believe their own words. Remember when I asked if you really believe that what you believe is really real? Well, the people in this movement don't.

Let's look at multiculturalism first. What could be wrong with this? Shouldn't we, as Christians, understand all cultures so that we may better be able to spread the gospel? After all, the apostle Paul wrote in 1 Corinthians 9:20–22:

> To the Jews I became like a Jew, to win the Jews. To those under the law I became like one under the law (though I myself am not under the law), so as to win those under the law. To those not having the law I became like one not having the law (though I am not free from God's law but am under Christ's law), so as to win those not having the law. To the weak I became weak, to win the weak. I have become all things to all men so that by all possible means I might save some.

Of course, Paul is correct. But that's not what the multiculturalists mean. They believe all cultures are equal. The Aztecs who cut out the beating hearts of human sacrifices were equal to the nominally Christian Spaniards who discovered this gruesome practice. Osama bin Laden's vision for a world culture based on Islamic fundamentalism is equal to that of our founding fathers'.

And because all cultures are equal, according to multiculturalists, none is better than another because there is no objective right or wrong. This means that there is no objective standard against which we can judge Montezuma, an al-Qaeda terrorist, or George Washington.

And this is where the multiculturalists slip in their true agenda. What they really mean by *multiculturalism* is that Western culture, based on a Christian worldview, is inferior to all others for the very reason that it claims that it is better than others. Not perfect, just better. (Winston Churchill once joked that democracy is the worst possible political system—until you consider all the others.) One reason I think multiculturalists recoil at this is Rule No. 5: *Christianity is dangerous to the world system.* The worldview on which Western culture was based—emphasis on *was*—makes moral claims on us. Many multiculturalists hate Western culture, although if you ask them why, they won't say anything resembling Rule No. 5. In fact, they can't even articulate where their hatred comes from. That's in line with Rule No. 4: *The ability of people to recognize truth diminishes the closer that truth is to their own heart, to the very nature of being a person.*

People who claim the superiority of one culture over another, particularly if it's based on a Christian worldview, blaspheme multiculturalists' twin gods—*diversity* and *tolerance*.

True diversity is what we find in the words to the children's song at the beginning of this chapter. But the multiculturalists mean that we must accept every worldview without question. And not only accept them, but affirm and celebrate them.

SELECTIVE MEMORY

Multiculturalists always talk about the bad things done by Western civilization—the Crusades, the Inquisition, etc.—without mentioning all the good things Western, Christian culture has introduced to the world. For example, the very concept of a university, meaning a unity to all learning, arises from the Christian worldview. Science as we know it today would not exist without its Christian roots. (More on that in chapter 13.) Hospitals, orphanages, universal education—indeed, the very concept of individual human rights—are uniquely Christian.

In fact, the freedom to carp and complain that the multiculturalists enjoy under our system of government would not exist if not for men who were deeply immersed in a Christian worldview. (More on that in chapter 7.)

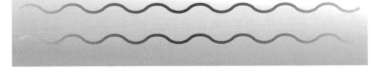

True tolerance is when I really don't like cabbage but I tolerate the smell when my wife cooks it. (She loves it!) That doesn't mean I like or approve of it. But that's not what multiculturalists mean by tolerance. They would force me to eat the cabbage, since my hating it is judgmental—more blasphemy to the multiculturalists. They really believe that we should not judge at all.

It is intolerant to say my religion is true and yours isn't. It is intolerant to say homosexual practices are deviant. Never mind any evidence that might be introduced to prove the point; you're being judgmental simply by saying one is better than another.

Francis Schaeffer said that as a culture evicts God, it must replace him with something. (More on that in the next chapter.) Some use political beliefs such as fascism, socialism, or communism. In our day people create a virtue of tolerance, a word that can mean anything they want it to mean. As writer Andree Seu says, "Tolerance is not (I cynically suspect) meant to be pinned down with hard facts, but to be elusive, watery, and weightless, so that it may inspire vague good will without the baggage of content."[1]

Do as I Say, Not as I Do

Notice that multiculturalists are intolerant of my intolerance. If they truly believed in tolerance, well, my being intolerant would be something to tolerate. But remember, they have changed the meaning of tolerance. If they want to celebrate diversity, as they're fond of saying, intolerant people should be but one hue in the colorful rainbow that is our world—one of their favorite metaphors, by the way. No such luck, though. They're being judgmental by judging your intolerance as something intolerable.

Leslie Armour, a professor at the University of Ottawa, once said, "Our idea of a virtuous citizen is to be one who tolerates everything but intolerance." And according to the United Nations' *Declaration of Principles on Tolerance*, "Tolerance . . . involves the rejection of dogmatism and absolutism"[2]—a view stated with absolute dogmatism.

46

As with most worldviews that have replaced Christianity, there are many internal contradictions. Tolerance and diversity are gods, and they're jealous ones. They demand that all bow before them. Thus, tolerance, over time, becomes intolerance. It's inescapable—at least in the way the multiculturalists define the term.

A symptom of all this is speech and behavior codes on college campuses that forbid any speech or action that might offend someone. (Indeed, many go out of their way to be offended.) Most multiculturalists are strong advocates of free speech—when it comes to criticizing anyone and everything that does not fall into line with their worldview. They're free speech advocates because it's crucial to their propaganda and need for control. But once they're in charge, their contempt for, say, the Christian worldview suddenly takes a dim view of free speech—for everyone but themselves, that is.

Another problem of multiculturalism is that it denies our common humanity. It is a direct offshoot of Marxism, in which people are not individuals but merely part of a class. It leads to a sort of tribalism: women against men; blacks against whites; gays against straights; third world against first world, etc. In fact, some people can belong to several favored groups at once.

This leads to preferential treatment for some—gays, blacks, Latinos, Native Americans, women—at the expense of others, a fundamental violation of fairness.

Multiculturalism, for political purposes, attempts to lump people together using irrelevant characteristics—e.g., skin color. That is the reasoning behind affirmative action: all black people must think alike, so to enforce diversity, we'll give blacks a leg-up for a job or a spot in an incoming law school class. Surprise, though. Not all blacks think alike, nor do all whites or any other ethnic group.

It's condescending too. Take this example: In 2003 Jeanne McDonnell, a freshman at the College of William and Mary, wanted to enroll in a five-week seminar called the Summer Transition Program, which offered to help students develop good study habits and test-taking skills. But the seminar was racially segregated. As a white woman, she was not allowed to enroll; only preferred

Two Wrongs Don't Make a Right

The impulse behind affirmative action is a good one. Certain groups were treated unjustly in the past. Slavery and the wars and duplicity our government practiced against Native Americans, for example, were evil. And righting an injustice to the individual who was wronged is just and right. That's why the U.S. government paid reparations to those Japanese-Americans who were sent to internment camps during World War II and why the German government paid damages to the actual survivors of the Holocaust.

But no one alive today was a slave or robbed of land in the Indian wars. To give a black person or Native American an unjust advantage over someone else because of what happened to his ancestors is just that—unjust. We as a society should try to help disadvantaged groups (and others). In a dead-even tie for a job position, an employer could decide to hire the black woman out of a desire to help a person from an underprivileged past. But to compel it by force of law is a violation of natural law. (More on that in chapter 6.)

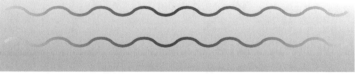

minorities were accepted. Think about the assumption behind this policy. Because some minorities struggle in school, all must therefore need help. As President George W. Bush said, it's the soft bigotry of low expectations.

This sort of tribalism has also led to voluntary segregation: separate graduation ceremonies, dorms, and clubs. Whatever happened to Dr. King's dream that everyone would be judged by the content of his character, not the color of his skin?

This favoritism—and condescension—can go to the extreme. Back in 1985 a Guatemalan woman wrote a book called *I, Rigoberta Menchu*. In it, she tells the story of the repression of the peasants in her country by the rich, white power elite. This book was a grand slam for the multiculturalists: it featured a dark-skinned woman from an oppressed class being put down by white males.

Based on her book, Ms. Menchu was awarded the Nobel Peace Prize in 1992. But then something funny happened. A researcher named David Stoll started checking into the details of Menchu's story, and almost all turned out to be either highly exaggerated or completely false. So did the Nobel committee revoke her prize? Did the multiculturalists who had uncritically accepted her story renounce her? Did the publisher withdraw the book? No, no, and no. Their basic reasoning was that Menchu's story *could* be true. And in fact there had been a lot of killing on both sides of the Guatemalan civil war. Menchu's book was actually a disservice, since it called into doubt all the other true reports of atrocities. That didn't matter. As Menchu herself said, anyone who challenged the truth of her book was motivated only by her race; they were racists for insisting on the truth.

In the end, multiculturalism denies the individual humanity of everyone. People are seen only as part of a race, region, socioeconomic group, and so on. They are not each an individual creation of God—no two alike, each with a unique gift. The philosopher Immanuel Kant said that we should never treat people as a means to an end, but as an end in themselves. By lumping people into categories based on skin color, ancestry, or whatever, they become a means to an end—usually a political goal. They are no longer people but things.

Multiculturalism also denies those things that unite us, those things that are common to the human experience. Take the arts, for example. The best writers and musicians capture this: Shakespeare and Homer are as relevant today as they were hundreds of years ago because of their ability to speak to the common human experience. But to many multiculturalists, these guys are little more than dead white males. (White males are at the absolute bottom of the multiculturalists' list of acceptable groups, and being dead means they have nothing to say to today's culture.)

That is why so much of what passes for good literature today is actually so banal and will not pass the test of time. It doesn't speak to what it means to be human as I discussed in the previous chapter; it speaks to what it means to be a member of a certain oppressed group at a certain period in time.

So What's the Problem?

Writer Josh McDowell outlines a few of the major implications of multiculturalism, tolerance, and diversity:

The death of truth: If all cultures are equal, and if all opinions are equal, then no one can make a claim to have the absolute truth.

The death of virtue: Why strive to be brave, honorable, or selfless if someone else can simply call these things cowardly, dishonorable, and selfish because he disagrees with your actions?

The death of justice: To make a claim that something is unjust is to assume some universal sense of justice. To the multiculturalist there's no such thing. Every idea is equal, so holders of all those opinions have an equal claim on us.

The loss of conviction: If every lifestyle and opinion is equal, you can no longer be convinced that your own lifestyle and opinions are correct. Indeed, "correct" is a meaningless term.

The privatization of faith: To make a claim of religious truth is to violate the idea of tolerance and multiculturalism. It's okay if you believe this stuff in the privacy of your own home, but don't take it into the public sphere.

The tyranny of the individual: Since everyone has a right to believe anything he wants, any single person can obstruct the rights of the majority by claiming his civil rights are being violated. If he disagrees with an idea, he can prevent that idea from being circulated, since there is no objective standard against which to measure his grievance. More on this in chapter 6.

The end of human rights: The Declaration of Independence of the United States asserts that people are endowed by their Creator with certain unalienable rights. If we cannot allow religious claims in public, and all cultures are equal anyway, who are we to condemn a country that jails its people for dissent or sells them off into slavery?

The exaltation of feeling: Why bother with marshalling facts and constructing a strong argument in favor of something if someone can merely denounce it because it violates his feelings? No need to use a standard available to everyone—for example, logic—if emotions are the ultimate trump card.

The exaltation of nature: As described in chapter 3, if humans have no inherent worth beyond that of an animal, we cannot make moral claims for, say, building a hospital to save human lives if doing so will interfere with the habitat of some obscure rodent. (Don't scoff—it happened near where I live.)

The descent into extremes: If all ideas and lifestyles are equally valid, there is no restraint on people who want to do extreme things, such as having a father have a sex-change operation so that he can become his children's "mother."[3]

As you can see, there's nothing harmless about the agenda of the multiculturalists.

5

Do the Right Thing

I once watched a TV magazine show that featured a man who had set up a special school in the heart of a poor inner-city neighborhood. It was apparent that this man was motivated by his Christian faith, but the host of that particular segment described him as a man who was "really in touch with his values."

Was the TV host so clueless that he couldn't understand what he was seeing? Or was he afraid to acknowledge that someone could be motivated by something absolute, something outside himself? I suspect it was the latter. We have reached a point in our culture where we're happy to talk about *values*—hey, everyone has values—but we seem to be afraid to consider *virtue*.

Many years ago the Greek philosopher Socrates asked, "Is an act right because God wills it, or does God will it because he knows it is right?" Such questions have long been a preoccupation with men. The very idea that we should do good and not do bad seems to be written on the human heart, an idea I will develop further in the next chapter in a discussion of natural law.

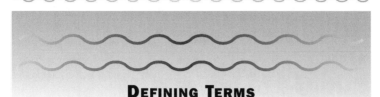

Defining Terms

Ethics describes the study of *morality*, which itself is concerned with questions of right and wrong. Ethics encompasses four major issues, which are perhaps best formulated by J. P. Moreland and William Lane Craig:[1]

1. A moral judgment must be accepted as an authoritative guide to actions, motives, and attitudes. (It cannot just be based on emotion or someone's personal opinion.)

2. A moral judgment must tell us what actions, motives, and attitudes we must have. It *prescribes* actions; it does not merely *describe* things. (Don't steal the cat vs. The cat has been stolen.)

3. A moral judgment must be able to be applied to all people at all times in all places in all similar situations. (It is always wrong to murder.)

4. Moral judgments are concerned with furthering human life, human dignity, the welfare of others, the prevention of harm, and the benefit of others. (Act toward others as you would have them act toward you.)

But for now, what are some of the ways men try to do the right thing and not do the wrong thing?

The Ethical Decision Tree

When it comes to making an ethical decision, some resort to nonrational means—consulting a Ouija board, their horoscope, or more often, simple emotion: "Don't do that! I hate it!" But most people at least try to use rational thinking. Sometimes they'll appeal to simple prudence: "Don't do that or you might hurt someone." (This begs the question of why it is wrong to hurt someone.) Most of the time, though, people will appeal to some sort of ethical principle.

Such appeals fall into two main categories: appeal to the consequences of an act or appeal to a higher principle. Under consequences, you might appeal to egoism, that is, do what is best for you. (This is not the same thing as egotism—the love of self.) You might also use a utilitarian calculation—trying to create the greatest good for the greatest number of people.

An appeal to a higher principle might take several forms, for example, rationalism. Rationalism is the belief that we can use the power of reason to find the moral thing to do. It could also appeal to some divine command or, closely related, natural law.

Think of the moral decision tree as looking something like this:

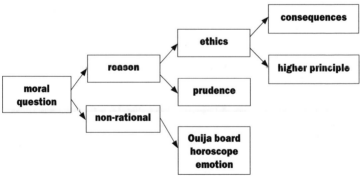

The first thing you might notice is that most of the time people jump around among these different elements, depending on what question they're trying to answer—or what action they're trying to justify. But as I said in the introduction, God has a funny way of hanging around, even if we don't want him to. This can be illustrated by the number of times different ethical theories smuggle in ideas that are incompatible with what they're really proposing. In effect, they don't really believe that what they believe is really real.

Please, Please Me

The principle of egoism is not as bad as it sounds at first blush. For example, an appeal to prudence for a given act is a form of egoism; you might hurt yourself. Giving money to the poor can also be a form of egoism; because doing this makes you feel good about yourself, such giving is the right thing to do.

The problem with egoism, though, goes all the way back to Rule No. 4: *The ability of people to recognize truth diminishes the closer that truth is to their own heart, to the very nature of being human.* A man may believe he's doing the right thing based on the principles of egoism, but can he trust his own inclinations?

Another fault of egoism is the tendency of taking it to an extreme. Homosexual activists appeal to a form of egoism to justify their sexual acts: It benefits me and doesn't hurt you, so I should do this. (They've smuggled in the idea that it is wrong to hurt people. That's because God's law is inescapable.) All sorts of other immoral actions are justified under the broad principle of egoism, all of which is made easier by the naturalistic worldview of evolutionary theory or the Freudianism I discussed in chapter 3. Abortion is justified on the grounds that it works to the benefit of the mother, never mind the life forming inside her.

Do the Math

Another ethical theory that hangs around in one form or another is utilitarianism. An act is right if it serves the principle of utility—creating the greatest happiness or greatest good for the greatest number of people. Like egoism, this is an ethical theory that appeals to consequences, not to higher principles.

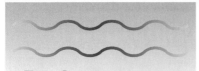

THE CONSEQUENCES OF IDEAS

The utilitarian philosopher Jeremy Bentham was strongly influenced by the Enlightenment's emphasis on empirical studies, using only the five senses to determine what is true. Another philosopher, David Hume, had studied society and ethics in a strictly empirical way and had come to the conclusion that the primary guides for men's actions were the passions. This is how Bentham got the pain-and-pleasure principle of utilitarianism.

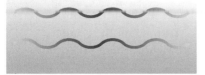

A form of utilitarianism was first proposed by Aristotle; he said that whatever leads to greater *eudaimonia* (Greek for happiness or well-being) is what is moral. The English philosopher Jeremy Bentham expanded on this in the nineteenth century. A lawyer as well as a philosopher, Bentham was troubled by a legal system that led to what he perceived to be gross injustices merely by an appeal to certain rights. (Here's another smuggling attempt: an appeal to something other than utility—justice, in this case.) Bentham wrote, "Nature has placed mankind under the governance of two sovereign masters, pain and pleasure. It is for them alone to point out what we ought to do."[2]

Utilitarianism had a certain appeal. If ethical decisions were based solely on standards that everyone could agree on, then moral conundrums would no longer exist, and no one could take advantage of others simply by declaring it was his right to do so, a part of England's not-so-distant past and the so-called divine rights of kings.

Bentham proposed a "hedonistic calculus" to determine the relative utility of action or nonaction of A over B. (Don't misunderstand his use of *hedonistic*; in that day it merely meant things pertaining to pleasure, not today's meaning of debauchery and libertinism.) By calculus, Bentham does not mean an upper-level math course. It's a method of computation, i.e., adding, subtracting, etc. It's calculating the various pains and pleasures, plus possible outcomes, in determining a course of action.

Critics immediately trashed Bentham's calculus, saying it could be used to justify man's basest desires; Bentham had no adequate response. But John Stuart Mill, who was strongly influenced by Bentham, thought he had an answer. He said the calculus dealt not only with quantity but also quality. He appealed to a higher concept of human happiness. Better to have prime rib than beef jerky. Better to listen to Mozart than the organ grinder on the corner. Mill wrote, "It is better to be a human being dissatisfied than a pig satisfied; better to be Socrates dissatisfied than a fool satisfied."[3]

Mill betrayed a certain upper-class bias, though. He said it was an "unquestionable fact" that people who are acquainted with both the "higher" and "lower" pleasures will show a "marked preference to the manner of existence which employs their higher faculties." His conclusions may have seemed perfectly obvious to a nineteenth-century English gentleman, but would they have been as obvious to a Japanese shogun living at the same time?

Mill did his own smuggling too. He used phrases such as "superior being" and "inferior being" to illustrate his ideas of qualitative vs. quantitative pleasure. But terms such as "superior" and "inferior" carry within them the idea of "good" and "bad," or "more preferable" and "less preferable." These terms assume a higher principle, something against which these ideas can be measured—a principle that cannot be found using a strict utilitarian calculus.

Utilitarianism has a lot more problems too. First, both Bentham and Mill believed that people automatically seek their own good—egoism, really—but it does not naturally follow that people would then seek the good of the larger society. In fact, it would be easy to make the opposite case; I'll seek my own good at your expense.

Later utilitarians appealed to "intuitive principles" such as justice and "rational benevolence." But once you allow intuitive principles, you are no longer within the empirical, testable realm of utilitarianism. In fact, Bentham had anticipated this. He believed that intuition was little more than one man foisting his own preferences on everyone else.

And what about secrecy? For example, you might violate a promise you made to your father on his death bed—let's say he wanted you to shave the neighbor's cat—on the grounds that doing so would create the greatest good for the greatest number. You don't keep your promise, thus avoiding traumatizing the neighbors when they find out that Puffy is no longer, well, puffy. But if it became widely known that you had lied to your father and did not keep your promise, then the principle of utility is violated because it would contribute to the decline of confidence in promise-keeping. Thus the same act would serve utility and violate utility at the same time, all on the basis of whether it is kept secret or not.

It is also assuming a lot to think that everyone would arrive at the same answer in doing the calculus. I may think X carries more weight than Y while you believe the exact opposite. To force an answer again becomes one man foisting his predilections on others. Then do you apply the calculus to individual acts or to society as a whole? What if I disagree? What rational, empirical principle will decide who's right? And besides, can we truly predict future actions or results? Much of the calculus assumes we can know exactly the ramifications of certain acts.

And how do we measure happiness anyway? I'm really happy watching a hockey game; my wife hates hockey. (Remember, she also *likes* cabbage!) So is utility being served if I'm happy and she's not? And I may then become less happy as my team takes a beating, while my wife's happiness goes up because she decided to cook herself some cabbage. Try to do the math—it's impossible.

The final problem with utilitarianism, though, is its view of human beings. All utilitarians believe people naturally seek their own happiness, and we should therefore try to create the greatest happiness for the greatest number. But what is it about people that we should care about their wishes? There's nothing in the supposed unbiased empiricism of utilitarianism that will lead us to that conclusion. It's more smuggling.

Moreover, I could easily come up with a utilitarian calculus that would create the greatest happiness by killing everyone over the age of fifty. If the numbers work out (assuming I could do the math in the first place), who's to say I shouldn't carry through with my idea?

And that's the deepest danger of utilitarianism. It denies any concept of human rights based simply on the premise that we're created in God's image—endowed by our Creator with unalienable rights, in the language of our founding fathers. Do you remember the Star Trek movie in which Spock goes into the engine room to fix some piece of equipment so that the ship won't be blown to pieces, even though doing so guarantees his death? As he dies, he does that Vulcan thing with his fingers and reiterates a line from earlier in the movie: "The needs of the many outweigh the needs of the few—or the one."

It sounds noble at first blush, but it's really a dangerous philosophy. Spock voluntarily went into the engine room—a selfless and noble act. But suppose Captain Kirk said he could save the ship by throwing everyone over the age of fifty overboard? The needs of the many outweigh the needs of the few, right? What about the rights of all those people about to be sucked into space? What if they didn't want to be tossed overboard? Too bad, according to utilitarianism. Remember, Bentham called the concept of rights "nonsense on stilts."

My example is silly, but real-life examples of this thinking abound today: euthanasia and human embryo research, for starters. These take some form of creating the greatest good for the

THE CATEGORICAL IMPERATIVE

The philosopher Immanuel Kant, in tune with his Enlightenment times, believed ethical decisions could be made on a strictly rational basis. In fact, reason was his highest principle. His categorical imperative reads like this: "Act only on that maxim through which you can at the same time will that it should become a universal law."

Some have misunderstood this to mean that Kant is actually appealing to the consequences of an act, not a universal higher principle such as reason. Their thinking goes like this: "I'd better not steal my neighbor's cat, because otherwise everyone will start stealing cats"— clearly an appeal to consequences of an action.

But that's not what Kant meant. Because reason and rationality were the ultimate higher principle for Kant, he would never appeal to consequences. The most famous example he gives for the categorical imperative is the "lying promise." He does not forbid the lying promise because it might lead to more lying promises, but because it was a logical contradiction—it was not rational. It would be like saying "four-sided triangle."

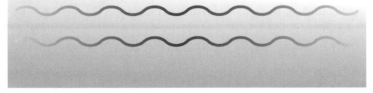

greatest number by killing a human being. Human rights don't enter into the calculation.

A form of utilitarianism often found today is called *pragmatism*. The right thing to do is what works. It's a very American creed; in fact, an American named John Dewey is often credited as the founder of pragmatism. Most of Dewey's work was in the field of education, but he famously said, "There are no eternal truths which are valid for this generation and succeeding generations—everybody has to find his own values in his own time."[4] That's when the word *values* entered our ethical lexicon, in the early part of the twentieth century. Pragmatism isn't a perfect match for utilitarianism—there's no calculus, for example. But it is similar in that any concept of right and wrong or human rights does not fit.

It's All Relative

Perhaps the most common form of ethical reasoning we are likely to encounter today is some form of *moral relativism*. This means simply that no objective standard for making ethical decisions exists. The right decision depends on who you are, what culture you live in, or what your personal beliefs are. (Smuggling alert: there's the word *right* again.) Moral relativism comes in three broad forms: *cultural moral relativism, personal moral relativism,* and *situational ethics.*

At first glance moral relativism seems to be a perfectly reasonable system. Don't impose your view on me, and I won't impose mine on you. One problem: that very statement is a form of imposing a view on someone. There's no such thing as a neutral position. Simply stating that a neutral position exists is not neutral—you've taken a position. (Like so many arguments that go against God's created order, they end up self-destructing.)

Fans of *Star Trek* might recognize this. Star Fleet's Prime Directive states that no one may impose a view on any planet or culture out there in space. Should the *Enterprise* find itself orbiting a planet where parents eat their firstborn children, Captain Picard

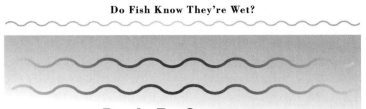

Don't Be Confused

Ethical reasoning can be described as a descending tree, with a broad theory at the top and moving down toward a specific decision—something like this:

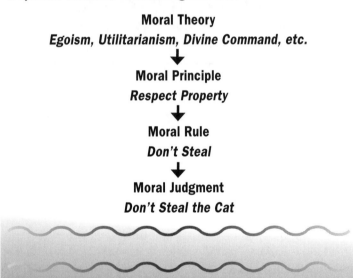

Moral Theory
Egoism, Utilitarianism, Divine Command, etc.
↓
Moral Principle
Respect Property
↓
Moral Rule
Don't Steal
↓
Moral Judgment
Don't Steal the Cat

could not tell the inhabitants that this was wrong or try to stop them. Many an episode was built around a potential violation of the Prime Directive, and one thing that never seemed to occur to the writers (and the characters they created) was that the very dramatic dilemma that made the show interesting resulted from them not really believing in the Prime Directive. They at heart understood that it was wrong to eat your firstborn. Moreover, the Prime Directive was not neutral. It was Star Fleet's position not to take a position, which is itself taking a position.

Moral relativism comes in a few different flavors. One states that moral rules are unique to a culture. Culture A eats its firstborn, and that's right for them. It's not for Culture B to judge them. But change the wording: Nazi Germany murdered Jews, and the United States had no right to judge their actions.

At first glance, it looks as if all the various cultures throughout history have had different moral values. This society believes life is sacred, that one believes suicide bombing is a high virtue. This one protects its unborn, that one kills its elders. If all these people believe such different things, there obviously can be no objective standard against which to judge their behavior.

Such thinking usually results from a confusion of rules and principles, as well as factual judgments. C. S. Lewis said that there has never been a culture that celebrated cowardice or rewarded treachery. Principles such as cowardice and treachery are universally shunned. Of course, history is full of cowards and betrayal; they just changed the rule. For example, our reasoning would be as follows:

Principle: *Bravery is better than cowardice.*
Rule: *Fight bravely.*
Judgment: *We won't retreat.*

But some might change the rules and do the following:

Principle: *Bravery is better than cowardice.*
Rule: *Run away so you can fight bravely another day.*
Judgment: *Get outta Dodge!*

The Nazis' reasoning was as follows:

Principle: *Protect society.*
Rule: *Fight anyone who threatens society.*
Judgment: *Build concentration camps to exterminate Jews.*

Our reasoning would be:

Principle: *Protect society.*
Rule: *All people deserve protection from government.*
Judgment: *We must fight tyranny.*

You can look at many justifications for cultural moral relativism and see where the confusion results. Whenever you hear someone making a claim for moral relativism, look for the higher principle they are missing: honor life, protect society, respect property, and so on.

Another fault of cultural moral relativism most people don't think about is what to do with reformers. If cultural moral relativism were true, everyone in a given society would be a conformist. But what to do with the Dietrich Bonhoeffers and Martin Luther Kings? These men stood against the cultural norms of their time—Nazism and segregation—and are considered heroes as a result. It is interesting that many of the same people who espouse cultural moral relativism are the same who will cite the civil rights record of Dr. King—abortion advocates, for example. I guess they don't see the contradiction.

Don't Tell Me What to Do and I Won't Tell You

The other form of relativism is personal moral relativism. What is moral for you is not necessarily moral for me. This is a variation of the postmodernist thinking I talked about in chapter 2. What's true for you is not necessarily true for me.

While cultural moral relativism might result from misunderstanding, it is hard to see how anyone could justify personal moral relativism on any other grounds than selfishness or nihilism. (In chapter 2 I discussed how nihilism—*nihil* is Latin for "nothing"—was a denial of the possibility of knowledge. In the moral realm it means a denial of any grounds for morality.)

Ravi Zacharias, a moral philosopher, tells about the time he was speaking in front of a group of elite students at Oxford University—the elite of the elite, if you will. Ravi asked a student, "If I take a baby and slice it open with a knife, would you say that was evil?" The student responded, "Well, I would say that I didn't agree with what you did, but I couldn't call it evil."

There was also the incident of a professor at a major American university who had spent an entire semester teaching her students that morality was relative and then was shocked at the end of the course when she found out that most of the students had cheated on the final exam. You can only shake your head at such ignorance. As C. S. Lewis said in *The Abolition of Man*, "We make men without chests and expect of them virtue and enterprise. We laugh at honour and are shocked to find traitors in our midst."[5]

Moral relativism is one reason I believe so many in Europe and some in the United States reacted so strongly to President George W. Bush when, after the terrorist attacks of 9/11, he said that this was a fight against evil. Many in post-Christian society are repulsed by any talk of moral absolutes implied in the use of the terms good vs. evil. It's also why some actually tried to *justify* what the terrorists did. It's Rule No. 5 at work.

Well, It Depends . . .

A form of relativism with a "kinder" face is situational ethics. This ethic does not deny right or wrong; the right choice, however, depends on the situation.

First proposed by Joseph Fletcher, situational ethics seeks to elevate people over rules and love over ethics. Believing that the Judeo-Christian view of morality was too rule-oriented, Fletcher said agape (Greek for self-giving, self-sacrificing love) should rule our actions. In fact, he mistakenly said situational ethics was what Christ taught, since he elevated love above the law.

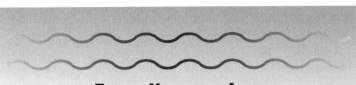

THREE KINDS OF LIES

Mark Twain said there are three kinds of lies: Lies, damned lies, and statistics. If he lived today, he might also add opinion polls. The rise of statistical polling in the last half of the twentieth century has led to a normalization of the abnormal. Let me explain: Politicians and news organizations are always taking polls. Some are innocuous: Are you going to vote for Candidate A or B? Do you think you're taxed too much?

But a lot of polling involves moral questions. Do you think abortion should be allowed? Should we allow homosexual marriage? Perhaps the precursor to all this came with the "findings" of Alfred Kinsey in the 1950s that supposedly showed that all sorts of sexual behavior society considered abnormal, if not immoral, was in fact happening with a large number of people. The implicit reasoning was that if more people than we thought were doing these things, they must be "normal."

And normal must mean it's right, no? This means statistics are being used to tell a lie. This is the fallacy of equivocation (more on that in chapter 16) that confuses two terms: normal and normative—that is, what most people are doing vs. what they should be doing.

President Bill Clinton believed this. In an interview with *Christianity Today* magazine, he said, "The approach to

66

specific moral issues in society should change as popular opinion changes."

It's unfortunate that many Christians fall for the statistical lie. We'll cite a poll that says X percentage of people think abortion is wrong, therefore it should be outlawed. In fact, it doesn't matter if only 1 percent of the population believes abortion is wrong, it should still be outlawed. The right thing to do is never subject to a popularity poll.

For a situationalist the ethical tree would look like this:

Principle: *agape*
Rule: *none*
Judgment: *Do the loving thing.*

The problem with situationalism is that it assumes no two situations are ever similar. In fact, there are a great many similarities between moral problems that rely on the same moral reasoning to solve them. Also, it's possible—almost certain, in fact—that three people of goodwill could still arrive at different answers to a given moral question.

Situationalists try to present themselves as principled relativists, and I'm sure they mean well. But Rule No. 4 is operative here. *The ability of people to recognize truth diminishes the closer that truth is to their own heart, to the very nature of being a person.*

Back to the Question

Remember that Socrates asked, "Is an act right because God wills it, or does God will it because he knows it is right?" The answer? None of the above, because it's the wrong question. Something is *right* if it is grounded in God's nature, and because we are created in God's image, we have the ability to recognize the right and, by extension, the wrong.

God has given clear guidance on right and wrong by writing his law on the human heart (Rom. 2:14–15). In the plainest sense, this is our conscience. Everyone has had an experience of his conscience telling him one thing while he does another. No one really has to tell us that it is wrong to murder. As I've said, the fact that people avoid being called a murderer is proof of this. I'll go into more detail on this in the next chapter.

God judges not just an act but also the heart—the motive behind it. For example, Jesus said in Matthew 5:28, "But I tell you that anyone who looks at a woman lustfully has already committed adultery with her in his heart."

To be sure, even Christians can face moral dilemmas. Should you lie to the Nazis at the door who are asking if you're hiding Jews? That one should be pretty easy to answer—the Nazis have no right to the truth in this case, and a greater harm would come if you told them that you had Jews hiding in your attic. Do you tell the telemarketer that your wife isn't home when she simply told you she didn't want to come to the phone? What if your boss asks you if you like his cat? Do you tell him the cat is fat and ugly, or do you commit a little white lie: "Well, that's some cat!" As Christians, we must rely continually on God's grace and forgiveness purchased at great price on the cross.

We must always force people to recognize the truth that they already know in their heart. As the prophet Isaiah warned, "Woe to those who call evil good and good evil, who put darkness for light and light for darkness, who put bitter for sweet and sweet for bitter. Woe to those who are wise in their own eyes and clever in their own sight" (Isa. 5:20–21).

6

Stop in the Name of the Law!

When I was growing up I liked watching cop shows on TV. Whenever the bad guy started to run away, the cops would pull out their guns and shout, "Stop in the name of the law!"

I assumed the crook knew that the law gave the cops the authority to yell that—not that he listened to them. He probably knew the law also said he couldn't rob the bank. Even if he had never seen the book that said, "It is against the law to rob a bank," he knew it was wrong. Otherwise, why run?

But how did he know this? How do we know it's against the law to rob banks, hit people over the head with a hammer, or steal someone's cookies?

To ask the most basic question, what is law? What gives it its authority?

What Is Good?

Very briefly, the law is something with authority behind it intended to make sure good things are protected and bad things are not allowed to happen. But such a definition assumes a more basic understanding of "good" and "bad."

Our Western culture is founded on natural law. In a way, all cultures are, but our Judeo-Christian heritage is—or *was*—based explicitly on this concept. It wasn't always that way. To see how we got from there to here, we need a brief history lesson.

Remember what Socrates asked? "Is an act right because God wills it, or does God will it because he knows it is right?" As with morality, law is a reflection of God's character. (Right now I'm not going to make a distinction between "law" as a general concept and "the law" given to the Israelites in the Old Testament; we'll soon see that they are basically the same.)

Simply put, this truth is the basis of natural law. Because we are created in God's image, we are able to recognize truth, fairness, and justice, as even a two-year-old recognizes when he's been treated unfairly. He doesn't have to be taught. He also doesn't have to be taught to quickly hide the cookie when Mom catches him with his hand in the cookie jar. As the police say, fleeing the scene of a crime is proof of an awareness of guilt.

We can see this sense of fair play, a sense of injustice, played out in the Bible. Notice what Job said as he underwent his trials. "Though I cry, 'I've been wronged!' I get no response; though I call for help, there is no justice" (Job 19:7). Note that God did not rebuke him for this complaint. Job believed he had done nothing to deserve what was happening to him. (Remember that word *deserve*; it will be important in a bit.) And he was right. God simply tells Job that he doesn't have all the facts. If he did, he'd realize he was not being treated unfairly.

All laws, even those not rooted in the Judeo-Christian tradition, have a sense of "oughtness" to them. In fact, the very idea of *ought* is proof of natural law. We all know at heart that we ought to do some things and not others. We can deny it or try to call it something else, but that is proof that it exists. You don't try to avoid made-up things.

This awareness appears throughout human culture. In the ancient Greek play *Antigone*, the heroine insists on the right to bury

70

her brother, Polynices, who was killed in battle, even though her uncle Creon has forbidden it. Antigone argues for a form of natural law by insisting it is the natural order of things that her brother be honored. She tells Creon that not allowing the burial is to tamper with "unwritten and unfailing laws, not of now, nor of yesterday; they always live, and no one knows their origin in time."

The Jewish culture of the Old Testament was steeped in laws of many types. Ceremonial law was about the proper way to worship God. It was also a foreshadowing of Christ's once-for-all sacrifice on the cross. Moral law was about relations between God and man as well as between man and man. Ancient Israel was a theocracy, meaning all the rules and laws were set by God. And from our Jewish roots, Christians should also have this strong understanding of law.

Both the ancient Greeks and Romans had a concept of law based on natural reason. In other words, a fair-minded person thinking clearly should be able to determine the right thing to do. It's the "fair-minded" part where we get into trouble, since sin has corrupted our ability to think fairly or objectively. Remember Rule No. 4? *The ability of people to recognize truth diminishes the closer that truth is to their own heart, to the very nature of being a person.* Because we are sinful, we are unable to see things objectively, especially when it comes to something that affects us. We may try, but there's always an element of "me" in our thinking.

Don't Think Positive

Law based on natural reason and not rooted in God's nature can lead in unpleasant directions. In medieval times, Christian theologians who were heavily influenced by the Greek philosophers, especially Aristotle, divided the law into two parts. The higher law of God was natural law. But based on Greek thinking, they also created a category of laws made by men, mostly laws governing civil conduct. This became known as positive law—but it was not a positive development.

71

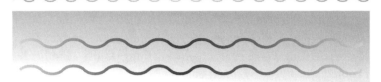

DIRECTIONS ARE THERE
FOR A REASON

Positive law is sort of like a certain episode of the TV show *Home Improvement*. Tim "the Tool Man" Taylor was trying to assemble a monster stereo system in his house, but he was running into one problem after another. His wife asked if he'd read the directions. "The directions are just the manufacturer's *opinion* about how to put this thing together," he answered. He finally finished and turned it on. The volume was set so high it blew out all the windows in the neighborhood, and he had no way of turning it down—or turning it off. When you ignore the "directions," such things can happen.

What's wrong with positive law? In a sense, nothing. We have many regulations that are not directly rooted in God's law. If Adam and Eve had never sinned, the Garden of Eden still would have eventually needed a traffic cop. But while there is nothing inherently moral or immoral about running a red light, the matter of obeying the appropriate civil authorities *is* a moral matter, so in a deeper sense, running a red light is an indirect violation of God's moral law. See Romans 13 for a better explanation of this.

The problem with positive law was that it became possible to sever law from God's authority—law founded in God's very nature. By the early 1800s, some legal philosophers influenced by the

72

Enlightenment came to believe that law was "mere opinion" about what men should do to live happy, just lives. (Without God's law, where did they even get the idea of *just*?)

Positive law had no underlying foundation. It was no longer rooted in things that all men can agree upon. But God has a tricky way of staying in the picture, because while most people today believe the law is anything we want to make of it, we still use words like *truth, justice,* and *fairness.* These concepts are not merely men's opinions; they are very real things. That's the way the universe is put together.

As long as there was still an echo of a Christian worldview in society, positive law generally tended to follow natural law. These people believed, naively, that everyone in all places at all times would believe and act like proper nineteenth-century Englishmen. It would be interesting to ask them how their concept of positive law would fare in Nazi Germany. And here's an important point. Under Hitler, killing Jews was not against the law. If the law is anything we say it is, then killing Jews (and unborn babies) is perfectly fine. If we truly believe in positive law, then we have no right to condemn the Nazis.

There again, natural law has a tricky way of staying in our hearts, even if we try to ignore it. It is part of our very beings, created in God's image, to seek justice and fairness in all things. Even the Nazis knew deep in their hearts that what they were doing was evil. That's why they hid their crimes behind a bland name, "The Final Solution." Doesn't sound so bad when you call it that, does it? The avoidance of a truth is the very proof of that truth.

Just Deserts

When our sense of justice is offended by a lawbreaker, we usually say something like, "He deserves to be punished."

But what do we mean by *deserve*? The word implies that there is a natural cause and effect between violating the "oughtness" of something and a necessary action to correct that violation, to set the balance right. In a sense, *deserve* is the same kind of word as *ought*. It's part of the very nature of natural law.

We react strongly when someone is punished if he didn't deserve to be, or if he's *not* punished when he ought to be. That's part of the appeal of cop shows. We root for the good guys because we want to see the crooks get what they deserve.

Today, however, the idea of punishment, or deserving something, is not being emphasized as much. It began in the late 1800s when well-meaning people changed the word *prison* to *penitentiary*. Because of the romantic worldview I mentioned in chapter 1, these people assumed that men were basically good, and for that reason criminals would realize the error of their ways and want to pay penance for their crimes. The sense that they *deserved* to be punished was lost.

You'll also hear that someone goes to jail to deter other people from committing the same crime. But if that is the only reason, why bother hunting down the criminal? You could simply pull someone off the street, throw him in jail, and say, "This is what will happen if anyone else breaks the law!"

"But that's not fair!" you shout. "The innocent person doesn't *deserve* to be thrown in jail."

You're right. It offends our sense of "oughtness" to punish the innocent. We punish someone for one reason only: because he deserves it. Without natural law, however, *deserve* has no meaning.

Throwing a criminal in jail may in fact deter others from committing the same crime, but that is only a secondary good effect. It should never be the primary reason.

The Cosmic "Says Who?"

Sometimes you'll hear someone say that if you don't believe in God, you can't be a moral person. This usually gets a rise out of atheists. They say they can be just as moral as anyone else.

And you know what? They're right, but they're missing the point. The question to ask is, Why bother? More to the point, what is "moral" if there's no standard to measure it against? How can something be called crooked if we don't have a concept of straight?

If there is no underlying reality to law, no ultimate enforcer of that law, there's no point in trying to be "moral." An atheist has no right to condemn anyone else, since without an ultimate standard, any condemnation is simply his own opinion.

People appeal to all manner of things to try to explain why some things are good and others bad. The simple question to ask is, "Says who?"

It's wrong to steal.

"Says who?"

It's wrong to hurt people.

"Says who?"

You see, they have the same fundamental impulses as you or I. They know it's wrong to steal, to murder, and to act unfairly or unjustly. They just can't explain where these concepts come from. Probably deep in their heart they suspect where these concepts are from, but they're committed to *not* believing in God. To stay intellectually consistent, they can't admit that. It's that old Rule No. 4 again.

The Russian writer Fyodor Dostoyevsky created the character Ivan in his masterpiece *The Brothers Karamazov*. In one scene, Ivan has a debate with the Grand Inquisitor, a character who represented the current world thinking with regard to law, morality, and religion. The Inquisitor makes the bold statement, "Without God, all things are permitted." He means this to be a good thing, but we, as well as Ivan, know it's a bad thing.

But the Inquisitor was right. Without God, all things are lawful. Without God, any time we judge someone guilty of breaking the law, we're merely stating an opinion formulated by some lawmaker or judge.

In the late 1800s the German philosopher Nietzsche boldly declared, "God is dead." He didn't mean that literally, since he didn't believe in God. What he meant was that the concept of God underlying law was dead. He was right. But this idea led to horrible

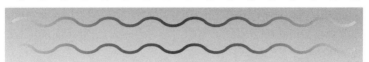

WITHOUT GOD, ALL THINGS ARE PERMITTED

Anytime someone claims that more people have been killed in the name of religion than any other cause, just remember Lenin, Hitler, Stalin, Mao Tse-tung, and Pol Pot of Cambodia. These men explicitly rejected the Judeo-Christian ethic, and together they account for more murders than the rest of history combined—about fifty million. Some horrible things have been done in the name of religion, but they don't hold a candle to what these men have done.

Sometime try renting the movie *The Killing Fields* about the rise of the communist Khmer Rouge rebels in Cambodia during the late 1970s. It is a perfect illustration of the abject terror and chaos that result from a completely lawless society that has rejected God. It's a world in which only the powerful—those with guns—rule. (Fair warning: this is a very violent, very brutal movie.)

A former aide to President Richard Nixon, Charles Colson, who served prison time for his part in the Watergate conspiracy, went on to found Prison Fellowship Ministries. He says that older prisoners today are terrified of the newer, younger men coming in. At one time even prisoners still had some sense of right and wrong, but the younger men raised in godless homes in a society that has largely rejected God do not have this sense. They are ruthless, without any moral sense whatsoever.

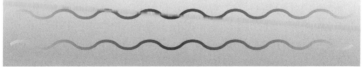

results—both the communist dictator Vladimir Lenin and Adolf Hitler were strongly influenced by Nietzsche.

It is our job to understand that law must be rooted in something outside itself to have any authority. Otherwise you can endlessly ask, "Says who?" when someone makes statements about right and wrong or legal and illegal. The ultimate answer is "Says God!"

This is an important concept to remember as our society races at ever faster speeds away from natural law. The United States Constitution is not a perfect document—originally black slaves counted as only three-fifths of a person—but it was written by men who still lived under the influence of Judeo-Christian law. They had a thoroughly Christian understanding of human nature—Rule No. 4 again—and formulated a document that took that into account.

Today our courts and political system are almost entirely dominated by men and women who take the concept of positive law as the normal state of affairs. Take this famous passage from a 1992 Supreme Court decision, *Planned Parenthood v. Casey*, which upheld a so-called constitutional right to abortion. The majority opinion, written by Justice Anthony Kennedy, said, "At the heart of liberty is the right to define one's own concept of existence, of meaning, of the universe, and of the mystery of human life. Beliefs about these matters could not define the attributes of personhood were they formed under compulsion by the State."[1] (Political philosopher Hadley Arkes said that "this is the kind of sentiment that would ordinarily find its place within the better class of fortune cookies."[2])

Think carefully about what Kennedy has written. We can define reality *any way we want to.* Taken to its logical conclusion, such thinking presents us with ridiculous choices. The more a society loses a consensus of what is true, what is lawful, or what is good, the more that society must be governed by increasingly detailed laws that try to take account of every human whim. Of course, they can never keep up, because once you pass one law, someone inevitably comes up with a way to dodge that law, resulting in yet another law, another dodge, on and on forever.

Another way to consider this is to look at our history. The farther we move away from ordered *liberty* (the freedom to be able to do the right thing) to *license* (the freedom to do anything, as in *licentiousness*), the more we see laws that allow homosexual marriage, legalized gambling, obscenity, and many other bad things.

Remember what the Grand Inquisitor said: "Without God, all things are permitted." If our society is to have any hope of surviving, we have to get God back into the picture.

7

You Can't Fight City Hall

I sat staring out the windshield of my car feeling really stupid. I was mad too. In my rearview mirror, I could see the police officer checking my car's registration, preparing to write a speeding ticket. I wasn't mad at him; he was the very model of professionalism and courtesy. I was mad at myself. I deserved this ticket, as much as I would have liked to make an excuse. (That's the problem with being mad at yourself; you can't find anyone else to blame.) I hadn't just drifted a bit over the speed limit, either. I was clocked more than 10 mph too fast.

Getting that ticket was an up-close-and-personal encounter with the power of government. But you encounter government every day. Look out your window. There's a road out there somewhere. That road has stop signs and traffic lights along it and police to patrol it. It might lead to the county courthouse or city hall. Stay on it long enough and it will take you to your state capital and, eventually, to Washington DC, our nation's capital. Above your house fighter jets may be patrolling the skies, and down the street there may be offices for military recruiters.

Government is inescapable. Someone has to be in charge if for no other reason than to keep all the cars from running into each other. Of course, government does a lot more than that. It's the ultimate arbiter of justice in a given society. (That doesn't mean that it's going to be *just* in the sense I describe in chapter 6.) It should be the enforcer of contracts, protector of the weak, and punisher of the guilty. It has the power to deprive people of life and liberty.

History shows us numerous forms of government across the world:

- monarchy (rule by the one, usually a king or queen)
- aristocracy (rule by the elite)
- oligarchy (rule by a small group for their own benefit)
- fascism (centralized dictatorship that allows no opposition, mixed with extreme nationalism)
- Nazism (fascism with a racist element thrown in)
- communism (no social or economic classes, all property is owned by the community)
- socialism (similar to communism, except ownership of industry can remain private)
- democracy (direct rule by all the people)
- republicanism (democracy in which the people elect representatives who govern with the consent of the people)
- libertarianism (the people have complete freedom with minimal interference by the government)

Many societies have had variations of the above and mix and match among them. Unfortunately, some cultures have experienced times when there was no government—anarchy, in other words. For example, in Judges 17:6, we read, "In those days Israel had no king; everyone did as he saw fit." It was not a good time in Israel's history.

Out of these forms of government, guess which one the Bible says is the best. None. The Bible never says anything about government

COWS AND GOVERNMENT

Here's an easy way to understand different types of government based on what they do with cows.

monarchy: You have two cows. The king takes some of the milk.

aristocracy: The ruling elite tells you what kind of cows to own and what to do with the milk.

oligarchy: Small ruling party tells you to raise their cows; they take all the milk.

fascism: You have two cows. The government takes them and denies they ever existed. Milk from any other country is banned.

Nazism: You have two cows. The government takes both and shoots you.

theoretical socialism: You have two cows. You give one to your neighbor.

real-word socialism: You have two cows. At first the government regulates what you can feed them and when you can milk them. Then it pays you not to milk them. After that it takes both, shoots one, milks the other and pours the milk down the drain. Then it requires you to fill out forms accounting for the missing cow.

theoretical communism: The cows belong to everyone. You take only as much milk as you need.

real-world communism: You have two cows. You give them to the government. The government gives you the amount of milk it says you need. If you don't like this arrangement, you "disappear."

anarchy: You have two cows. You steal a few more cows. Your neighbor hits you on the head with a brick and steals your cows.

libertarianism: Milk the cows and keep the milk for yourself; you hope the populace can find milk elsewhere.

democratic capitalism: You have two cows. You sell one and buy a bull.

except to obey it. The apostle Paul wrote, "Remind the people to be subject to rulers and authorities, to be obedient, to be ready to do whatever is good" (Titus 3:1). He also wrote,

> Everyone must submit himself to the governing authorities, for there is no authority except that which God has established. The authorities that exist have been established by God.
>
> Consequently, he who rebels against the authority is rebelling against what God has instituted, and those who do so will bring judgment on themselves.
>
> For rulers hold no terror for those who do right, but for those who do wrong. Do you want to be free from fear of the one in authority? Then do what is right and he will commend you. For he is God's servant to do you good. But if you do wrong, be afraid, for he does not bear the sword for nothing. He is God's servant, an agent of wrath to bring punishment on the wrongdoer.
>
> Therefore, it is necessary to submit to the authorities, not only because of possible punishment but also because of conscience. This is also why you pay taxes, for the authorities are God's servants, who give their full time to governing.
>
> Romans 13:1–6

Keep in mind that Paul was writing at the time when Nero was the Roman emperor. Nero was one of the most evil rulers in the history of the Roman Empire. I have to admit I find it puzzling that God would want us to submit to the likes of Nero, but that's what it says in the passage above.

So while the Bible never indicates a preferable form of government, we can figure out what type might best help us live the life that Christ commands us to live.

Give unto Caesar

A first principle to establish is that we do not owe the government what we owe to God. If the government tells us to do something contrary to God's word, we have a duty to disobey. As

Peter told the temple guards who had ordered the apostles to stop preaching the gospel, "We must obey God rather than men!" (Acts 5:29). Some have taken that to mean that they are never to obey the government, but Paul's passage above should quickly put that notion to rest.

The government does, however, have a legitimate right to require our obedience to the law. For example, on the issue of paying taxes, Jesus said, "Give to Caesar what is Caesar's, and to God what is God's" (Matt. 22:21). If I had told the police officer writing the ticket, "I'm part of the kingdom of God, not yours, so I don't have to obey your traffic laws," I probably would have been hauled off to jail—and rightly so.

The problem comes when government tries to take over duties that rightfully belong to individuals, families, or the church, something we see with increasing frequency today.

Let me explain. Our society exists as several spheres: family, church, school, community, and work. These spheres overlap: For example, I have a family, my kids go to school, we belong to a church, we live in a certain city, and I have a job. But each sphere has defined roles and responsibilities, as well as defined authority. Throughout, there are consequences for disobedience. And each sphere operates under God's moral law.

For example, the Bible spells out roles and responsibilities for elders and others within the church. The first chapter of Titus describes the requirements for an elder. The Bible describes the roles and responsibilities within a marriage and between parents and children. The passage from Paul cited above tells us what our duties are toward government and government's authority. When one sphere starts to intrude into another, though, taking for itself rights—and duties—that rightfully belong to the other, it begins to overstep its bounds. For example, if my boss tells me what church to attend and how to raise my children, he has overstepped his authority. We see this increasingly in government in Western culture.

83

A BRIEF HISTORY OF GOVERNMENT

Much of what we could call the Western tradition of government originated in ancient Greece and Rome and from Judaism and the Christianity that grew out of it.

The Greeks introduced the idea of the *polis* to the world—the city-state in which citizens participated directly in government. (That's where we get the word *politics*.) The Roman Republic was much like the Greek system, but it introduced the idea of law that was binding on all people living under Roman jurisdiction—foreigner, citizen, senator, or emperor. In fact, citizens had certain rights against the Republic, which the apostle Paul, as a citizen of Rome, took advantage of, demanding his right to a trial before Caesar.

As Europe became Christianized, respect for life and for the individual increased. For example, under feudalism, the peasants had certain duties toward the lord—providing food, for example—but he also had certain duties toward them, particularly protection.

The next major event in the creation of modern Western government came in 1215, when English nobles forced King John to recognize certain rights of the nobles. From there it was not a long step to the creation of England's constitutional monarchy, with a king or queen overseeing two houses of Parliament—the House of Commons and the House of Lords.

But if we had to pin down one event that has most contributed to our form of government, it would have to be the Protestant Reformation of the sixteenth century. Out of the Reformation grew the idea that just as individuals had a direct line to God without any earthly mediator, such as a priest or bishop, every man should have the right to have a say in how his government was run.

Various political philosophers put their own imprint on this idea, but the one who probably most affected the founding fathers of the United States was John Locke, who said that all men had a right to "life, liberty, and property." The founders, of course, changed that to "life, liberty, and the pursuit of happiness."

None of Your Business

The rise of the welfare state in the early part of the twentieth century, first in Europe, then in the United States, created a government that began to take authority over all these spheres. While the Bible clearly says that it is our duty as Christians to take care of the poor, the government took over that duty. For that reason, many have lost the notion that it is up to individuals to care for the downtrodden. Sure, many people donate money to food banks or work in soup kitchens, and those are good deeds, but most of society simply regards such services as the government's responsibility. This can create an entitlement mentality among the poor—"You owe me!"—that is the opposite of the Bible's injunction that anyone able to work who does not will not eat. It's also significant that in

85

those places with the highest level of government support for the poor, giving to charities and churches is the lowest.

During the summer of 2003, Europe suffered through a historic heat wave. In France, fifteen thousand people died of heat-related injuries, most of them elderly people. Sixty years of socialism had produced a society in which no one took responsibility for looking after his neighbors, even when the government was clearly overwhelmed by the crisis. Most of these people died alone. When we have heat waves in the United States, some people die, but these tend to be the shut-ins who have no family or friends to care for them. What is significant, though, is the number of neighbors who call authorities to report someone who might need help, the number who take in people who do not have air conditioning, and the number of companies that donate fans and air conditioners. You'll rarely find such giving in a country that has ossified into a socialist mentality.

The Bible also tells us it is our job to discipline and educate our children. Now I'm not saying everyone should homeschool and that all public schools are bad. Not everyone has the ability to homeschool or the money to send their children to a private Christian school. And many public schools are quite good. But how many families leave it up to the school to teach their kids everything, from math to science to religion? As a minimum, we must be the primary foundation for our children's education, and we must equip our children to be discerning and to think critically about what they're being taught in school. This goes for Sunday school and youth group too. It is not the church's job to teach kids everything they need to know about living as a Christian; it must start at home.

Where the government does the most damage, however, is when it starts to intrude into the parents' right—and responsibility—to raise their own children, and when it interferes in what the church may or may not do.

Many countries already have laws against spanking. In a well-intended attempt to try to stop child abuse, the state has taken from parents a legitimate form of discipline. And recently in Colorado, a state judge outrageously told a Christian mother to "make sure that there is nothing in the religious upbringing or teaching that the minor child is exposed to that can be considered homophobic." The case arose when a lesbian in a relationship with another woman became a Christian and renounced her lesbianism. The other woman sued for joint custody of the child, even though she had no legal or biological relationship with her. The judge granted this request, giving the Christian mother the order above. (He put no restriction on the lesbian woman about teaching the girl negative things about Christianity.) That is a case of the state very clearly intruding into an area in which it should have no authority.

In Nebraska, a state senator said, "We [the legislature of Nebraska] don't think [Christian parents] should be entitled to impose decisions or religious philosophies on their children which could seriously undermine those children's ability to deal in the complicated world when they grow up."

Finally, the rise of so-called hate crime laws also threatens to silence the church in the areas of sex and homosexuality. In Canada, for example, some American Christian radio broadcasts dealing with these topics are either heavily censored or not allowed to be broadcast at all. And a pastor giving a sermon on the biblical teaching about homosexuality could be charged with a crime if a gay person felt threatened.[1]

A New God

The rise of naturalism over the last 150 years or so reached most Western governments in the 1920s and 1930s. The pace has accelerated, however, over the past thirty years. Remember, naturalism teaches that there are no absolute truths, no spiritual realm, and no religious underpinnings to anything.

Cultural observer John Whitehead wrote, "The position of the American state is increasingly that of pagan antiquity, in which the state as god on earth provides the umbrella under which all institutions reside. Religion is thus a department of the state, as

87

is all else."[2] In fact, we face a form of religious war. The modern secular state is a jealous god, and it will tolerate no rivals. Hence, its war against Christianity.

That's why so many secularists are quick to cite a so-called "separation of church and state." First of all, no such phrase appears in the U.S. Constitution, and no courts believed there was any such thing until 1949. That phrase originates in a letter that Thomas Jefferson wrote to the Baptists in Danbury, Connecticut, assuring them that government would not interfere in their affairs. It has now been distorted to mean religion cannot interfere in any way with the functioning of government.

Would Jefferson agree with this interpretation? Well, let's hear what he had to say about the issue of religious faith and government: "And can the liberties of a nation be thought secure when we have removed their only firm basis, a conviction in the minds of the people that these liberties are the gift of God? That they are not to be violated but with his wrath? Indeed I tremble for my country when I reflect that God is just: that his justice cannot sleep for ever."[3] (You can find a lot more evidence of the Christian underpinnings of our nation at www.wallbuilders.com.)

The secularists use this alleged separation not only to deny any religious or moral underpinning for our law, but to push religion, particularly Christianity, out of the public square. As Christians and citizens, we cannot allow this. This goes beyond the United States too. Increasingly, international organizations such as the United Nations are trying to steal rights that properly belong to parents or church—for example, the U.N. advocates that children of any age have a right to engage in sex without their parents' permission, and with that "right" comes a right to birth control or abortion.

As I've described earlier, the very concept of rights depends on natural law. Instead of arguing for positions based on polls or pragmatic grounds, we must stress that a certain position is correct because it is in accord with the way God created the universe. At the same time, we must be humble enough to recognize that on some positions—say, tax policy—there is no necessary "Christian" position. People of goodwill can disagree on such matters. The task is to find which position works best.

But on issues of the rightful place of each sphere as I described above, we must not give ground. When the government tries to take away rights that God has granted to us, we have a duty—indeed, a right as citizens—to fight the government taking away what God has given us.

8

To Have and to Hold

Several years ago I attended a wedding in Cornwall, England. It was a beautiful ceremony in an old country church. The couple had asked a friend to do the Bible reading, and they chose a passage one hears frequently at weddings: 1 Corinthians 13:1–8.

If I speak in the tongues of men and of angels, but have not love, I am only a resounding gong or a clanging cymbal.

If I have the gift of prophecy and can fathom all mysteries and all knowledge, and if I have a faith that can move mountains, but have not love, I am nothing.

If I give all I possess to the poor and surrender my body to the flames, but have not love, I gain nothing.

Love is patient, love is kind. It does not envy, it does not boast, it is not proud. It is not rude, it is not self-seeking, it is not easily angered, it keeps no record of wrongs.

Love does not delight in evil but rejoices with the truth. It always protects, always trusts, always hopes, always perseveres.

Love never fails.

A funny thing happened. The friend chose an older English translation to read from in which the word *charity* is used in place of *love*. The bride and groom were very upset. Their reaction was a perfect illustration of what is wrong with marriage these days.

The word *charity* actually better describes what the apostle Paul meant in this passage. The Greek word is *agape*, which is the self-sacrificing kind of love exemplified by the life of Christ. Charity at one time carried this connotation, not today's meaning of giving money to the poor. And that being the case, this translation is still perfect to read at weddings.

But too many people today regard love, especially as used in 1 Corinthians 13, as a mushy affair, kind of a sloppy agape. In fact, their definition is closer to the Greek word *eros*, meaning a physical, sexual love. This is where we get our word *erotic*. And, according to this thinking, when you "fall out of love," well, then it's time to call off the marriage. In other words, when you're no longer physically attracted to your spouse, when the two of you are no longer compatible, it's time for a divorce.

In God's Image

Like so much in the world, a human institution should be rooted in God's nature. As with natural law, an understanding of God will help us understand marriage.

God exists as a trinity—three persons in one Godhead: Father, Son, and Holy Spirit, and they have always existed in eternal fellowship. It is difficult for the human mind to grasp this reality, but this doctrine is clearly taught in Scripture even if the word *trinity* never actually appears. And once you contemplate the Trinity, it helps explain a lot.

Think of it this way: one is alone, two is relationship, and three is fellowship. Four adds nothing to this, nor does it take anything away. In other words, the minimum number for fellowship is three. Also important is that aloneness is contrary to the nature of God. That's why God said it was not good for man to live alone and why he created woman to be his partner. For this reason, the ideal marriage consists of husband, wife, and God. And that's what the first marriage was, as we read in Genesis.

When you understand marriage in this way, it helps explain why divorce is contrary to God's perfect plan. "'I hate divorce,' says the LORD God of Israel" (Mal. 2:16). It is a ripping apart of something God has joined. As Jesus said, "Haven't you read . . . that at the beginning the Creator 'made them male and female,' and said, 'For this reason a man will leave his father and mother and be united to his wife, and the two will become one flesh'? So they are no longer two, but one. Therefore what God has joined together, let man not separate" (Matt. 19:4–6).

Something about the sexual act brings this about, whether or not you're married. The apostle Paul wrote, "Do you not know that he who unites himself with a prostitute is one with her in body? For it is said, 'The two will become one flesh'" (1 Cor. 6:16). That's why sex outside of marriage is so damaging. It is creating a one-flesh body that is not intended to last. Despite the happy-go-lucky image of swinging singles hopping in and out of bed, people who live like this are lacking something, and they realize it. They keep looking for fulfillment in all the wrong places. Even the racy TV show *Sex and the City* wound up reaffirming the biblical view of sex, with all of the main characters eventually getting married or longing for a husband. (They wouldn't admit it that way, however. Rule No. 4 again.)

In addition to making marriage something based only on feelings, our culture has stripped it of any transcendent truth. It has become little more than a legal contract that's relatively easy to break. And usually the biggest losers are women. The woman is often left to raise children without benefit of a husband and the security and income that means. And even outside of marriage, the sexual license that has become part of our culture hurts women almost exclusively. Women have become prey for predatory men in the sense that once they are no longer of use, so to speak, they're discarded with absolutely no moral or legal repercussions. (As grandmothers of old used to say, "Why buy the cow when you can get the milk for free?")

IT'S GOOD FOR YOU TOO

As with so many things that are part of God's created order, marriage is good for you—and your children. Numerous studies show that married men live longer than single men; the same is true for women. Children raised in the same home as their parents do better on every psychological and sociological scale.

On the other hand, children of divorce may experience many challenges and insecurities not shared by their friends from intact homes. Surprisingly, even those children raised in a single-parent home that has resulted from the death of mother or father do better than those in divorced families; that's because the missing parent is still honored and the children do not sense that they were abandoned.

In "The Stakes: Why We Need Marriage," Maggie Gallagher writes: "The consequences of our current retreat from marriage is not a flourishing libertarian social order, but a gigantic expansion of state power and a vast increase in social disorder and human suffering. The results of the marriage retreat are not merely personal or religious. When men and women fail to form stable marriages, the first result is a vast expansion of government attempts to cope with the terrible social needs that result."[1] And, as I noted in the previous chapter, the inevitable result is government forcibly taking on rights and responsibilities that rightfully belong to families and parents.

Political commentator Sam Schulman has great insight on this, which is worth quoting at length:

> Marriage can only concern my connection to a woman (and not to a man) because . . . marriage is an institution that is built around female sexuality and female procreativity. (The very word "marriage" comes from the Latin word for mother, *mater*.) It exists for the gathering-in of a woman's sexuality under the protective net of the human or divine order, or both. This was so in the past and it is so even now, in our supposedly liberated times, when a woman who is in a sexual relationship without being married is, and is perceived to be, in a different state of being (not just a different legal state) from a woman who is married. . . . A woman can control who is the father of her children only insofar as there is a civil and private order that protects her from rape; marriage is the bulwark of that order. . . . For a woman, the fundamental advantage of marriage is thus not to regulate her husband but to empower herself—to regulate who has access to her person, and to marshal the resources of her husband and of the wider community to help her raise her children.[2]

Some consider marriage oppressive, likened to slavery, or believe marriage benefits only men. For instance, the "Declaration of Feminism," written in 1971, says: "Marriage has existed for the benefit of men and has been a legally sanctioned method of control over women. . . . We must work to destroy it."[3] (By the way, in tossing out a God-designed institution, this type of feminism leads inevitably to paganism. That same Declaration says one way to avoid the "oppression" of marriage is to "go back to ancient female religions [like witchcraft]." Compare that statement to the rise of witchcraft and so-called "goddess" religions today.)

Gay "Marriage"

Another inevitable result of turning marriage into merely a legal contract is opening the door to homosexual "marriage." I put that word in quotation marks because, as Schulman states above, the term inherently carries with it a sense that it is for the protection of women.

Gay activists say it is a fundamental matter of fairness that they get the same "rights" that heterosexual marriages enjoy, such as filing joint tax returns, inheritance rights, hospital visitation, and the like. But a fundamental principle of fairness, one largely lost today, is that you treat things that are alike the same and those that are unlike differently. No matter what you call it, two homosexuals posing as a family are not a family, despite what some say.

Take, for example, the book written by former Vice President Al Gore and his wife, Tipper. Called *Joined at the Heart: The Transformation of the American Family*, the Gores start by saying, "For us, as for most Americans, family is our bedrock, and we believe the strength of the American family is the nation's bedrock."[4] They then undermine everything they purport to believe about families by defining *family* as "getting beyond words, legal formalities, and even blood ties."[5] In other words, family is anything you say it is: polygamy, polyandry, or gay marriage.

But marriage must have a fixed meaning if it is to mean anything at all. (See more on such wordplay in chapter 12.) Society blesses marriage with many benefits such as tax deductions or inheritance rights for precisely the reason that it regards (or regarded) families as important as the fundamental building block for a stable society and for the protection of women and children.

Even childless marriages protect this purpose, says Maggie Gallagher, by ensuring that, as long as the marriage exists, neither the childless husband nor the childless wife is likely to father or mother children outside of wedlock. (This is an important point, because gay activists usually cite childless marriages as proof that the primary purpose of marriage is not about children.)

If we redefine marriage to mean anything, Gallagher says, "Marriage will no longer be a carrier of the message that children need mothers and fathers. Instead, the law will legitimate the principle of family diversity: that adults get to form the families they choose and children will resiliently adjust. Or not, but who cares?"[6]

GIVEN OVER

Perhaps the Bible's definitive statement about homosexuality comes in the first chapter of Romans. The apostle Paul clearly links homosexual activity to a form of idolatry.

If you think of the marriage relationship in the trinitarian way I describe above, as a fellowship of different persons, you'll see why homosexuality does not fit within this definition. When God said in the Garden that it was not good for man to be alone, he did not create for him another man. God created a being who would *complement* man. Males and females complete each other. Anyone who's been married can tell you that his spouse has many traits quite different from his.

Two men cannot replicate this relationship because they *don't* complement each other; they're both fundamentally the same thing. In order to have a romantic relationship, one must become what he is not—a woman. The opposite is true for lesbians. In other words, homosexual relationships are a perversion of God's created order.

And anyone not blinded to truth can see that even in the physical realm, men and women complement each other; the "plumbing" fits, in other words. Homosexual acts are nothing but a degraded imitation of this.

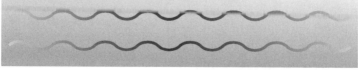

This is the reality: marriage exists regardless of law. Laws merely serve to set the boundaries and keep the public meaning of marriage. Schulman writes, "Without this shared, public aspect, perpetuated generation after generation, marriage becomes what its critics say it is: a mere contract, a vessel with no particular content, one of a menu of sexual lifestyles, of no fundamental importance to anyone outside a given relationship."[7]

While society has a great stake in protecting traditional marriage and families, it has no stake in protecting gay "marriages." Whether or not gays remain monogamous is of no concern to society. (Indeed, many studies show that even in "long-term committed relationships," gays have many sexual partners.) In fact, the more honest gay activists readily admit that the reason they push for gay marriage is precisely to destroy what they consider a bourgeois, oppressive institution.

The gay rights movement in fact tries to redefine the very nature of sexuality. Rather than the inescapable fact that we are created male or female (Gen. 1:27), they want to redefine the sexes by *behavior* or *self-perception.* You'll notice in talk of the so-called GLBT (gay, lesbian, bisexual, transgendered) movement, there is no fixed definition of gender. You are what you perceive yourself to be. For that reason, men should be allowed to dress like women and vice versa, and denying them employment, for example, on this basis is considered rank discrimination.

The stakes could not be higher. Taking sex out of the transcendent realm and turning it into mere recreation has led to innumerable societal problems.

9

Art for Art's Sake

A person should hear a little music, read a little poetry and see a fine picture every day in order that worldly cares may not obliterate the sense of the beautiful which God has implanted in the human soul.

—Goethe

I worked in midtown Manhattan for several years during a time when the city was trying to clean up its graffiti-plagued subway system. The cars would be literally covered from top to bottom, front to back with brightly colored vandalism. It sounded sensible that New York City would try to prevent this defacement and clean up the cars. Except that the plan met with outrage from the "artistic" community. As one woman put it, "I don't ever want to be in a position of judging someone else's art."

How had we come to the point where public vandalism was considered art? And more to the point, how had we arrived at the place where it was bad form to judge another's "art"?

Before answering that, though, let's back up a bit: What is art in the first place? Is it just beautiful paintings and sculptures at the local art museum? Can only aesthetically sensitive people create art? Do you need a special education to appreciate art?

No, no, and no. Our word *art* has the same Latin root as *artisan,* *artifact,* and *artificial,* and all carry the connotation of something made by man. We are creators. Because we're made in God's image, we have an innate need to create.

It's in Our Genes

Have you ever picked out new curtains? Painted your living room? Built a bookshelf? Then you are, in the strictest sense of the word, an artist. In fact, art is inescapable. Choosing the fabric and color of those curtains was an aesthetic decision. So was choosing the texture and color of the paint. And even if the bookshelf is nothing more than pieces of plywood fashioned together, the very decision to make it plain was an aesthetic decision. The question is not shall we have art, but shall we have *good* art. An understanding of this should affect the way we live our lives—something I'll come back to in a bit.

For now, however, let's look at God's view of art. Beauty is an essential part of God's nature. The psalmist wrote, "One thing I ask of the LORD, this is what I seek: that I may dwell in the house of the LORD all the days of my life, to gaze upon the beauty of the LORD and to seek him in his temple" (Ps. 27:4). The apostle Paul assumes we have the ability to recognize what is aesthetically good when we see it: "Finally, brothers, whatever is true, whatever is noble, whatever is right, whatever is pure, whatever is lovely, whatever is admirable—if anything is excellent or praiseworthy—think about such things" (Phil. 4:8).

Look at the directions God gives to Israel in the book of Exodus for making the ark of the covenant, the tabernacle, the priests' robes, and other such things. The details are intricate, the materials of the highest quality. This is a true craftsman at work.

Take, for example, this passage: "[The ephod's] skillfully woven waistband is to be like it—of one piece with the ephod and made with gold, and with blue, purple and scarlet yarn, and with finely twisted linen" (Exod. 28:8). The artisans who were to make these things are the first people in the Bible described as being filled with the Holy Spirit.

Christians are people of the word and the Word (see John 1). God has chosen to communicate with us through the written word, but he has also chosen to use art—music, images, poetry—to help communicate these truths. The rainbow was a piece of art, used to illustrate God's promise to Noah.

Unfortunately, what to do with art has been an ongoing struggle in the church. After the split of the Roman Empire between Rome and Byzantium (later Constantinople), the two parts of the church fought over the use of icons in worship. The East used them; the West thought they were idolatry. Even within the Eastern church a movement arose whose followers destroyed icons wherever they found them. (That's where we get the word *iconoclast*: a smasher of icons.) But just because Rome disapproved of icons doesn't mean it didn't have ideas about art. Just look at the beautiful illuminated manuscripts of the Bible created during the Middle Ages. The population was largely illiterate, but the stories of the Bible were communicated through these beautiful illustrations. And the Vatican is one of the largest owners of fine art in the world.

So What Is Art?

But most people's idea of art is the visual arts and, more precisely, the fine arts. In other words, even though art is an everyday part of life, most discussions center on these categories.

To understand art, we need to focus on two key concepts: *form* and *content*. Form is simply what medium or form is used to create the piece: paint, wood, clay, plaster, and so forth. Content is what the piece is saying, what idea it is trying to communicate.

You've probably heard it a hundred times: beauty is in the eye of the beholder. Is that true? Sure, most people have a subjective reaction to a piece of art, but does that mean artistic standards are merely subjective? No. We need to learn artistic norms so that we are not restricted to only our subjective experience when we confront art. In other words, beauty is *not* in the eye of the beholder.

The Greek philosopher Aristotle was perhaps the first to formulate the transcendent norms of beauty. (Remember Rule No. 2: *God is the God of truth. All truth is God's truth.*) Aristotle said the factors common to the beautiful are:

- *Proportionality: portraiture vs. a stick figure.* The *Mona Lisa* vs. a child's kindergarten drawing.
- *Harmony: symphony vs. cacophony.* The Chicago Philharmonic vs. a construction site.
- *Simplicity: simple vs. simplistic.* A Gregorian chant vs. "Happy Birthday."
- *Complexity: epic poetry vs. doggerel.* Homer's *Iliad* vs. a limerick.

With this understanding, you should be able to take the first steps toward understanding art—visual, musical, dramatic, and its many other forms. Gene Edward Veith provides a good example of critiquing both form and content with the classic Velvet Elvis. You've probably seen some variation on this—a soulful Elvis Presley portrait painted on black velvet, usually sold by some roadside vendor.

The black velvet painting of Elvis is aesthetically bad, among other reasons, because the form and the content simply do not go together. To make a quasi-religious icon to a rock and roll star is incongruous to begin with. . . . Further, the attempt to praise Elvis is subverted by the material, which, for all of black velvet's pretensions to elegance, is actually cheap and tawdry. . . . The idealization of the image, the larger-than-life soulful eyes, the stylized sexiness jarringly combined with other-worldly reverence . . . also subvert the effort to honor a real person. The other faults of the work—its sentimentality, clumsy drawing, washed-out coloring, and superficiality of detail—are failures of form.[1]

Art vs. Idolatry

Many people, when hearing the word *art*, immediately think of some form of art that represents a real thing in the world—say, a king, a cat, or a cabbage. Does that mean then that such representational art is idolatry as defined in the second commandment?

A lot of Christians have believed so, but I don't believe that's the case. As always, God judges the heart, not the external action. If you make a sculpture of your cat and bow down to worship it, then it's clearly an idol. But if you make the same sculpture because you enjoy working in clay and making pretty knickknacks for your living room, then it's simply art, not idolatry. The first sculpture could be executed excellently and the second amateurishly, but in this case content (and intent) count more than form.

After the Protestant Reformation, some reformers smashed stained-glass windows and statues out of an extreme reaction against Rome; they demanded that churches have no decoration or art in them. They were, I believe, confusing content and form. A stained-glass window can tell a biblical story, or it can be beautiful for its own sake. Or you could create statues of Mary and Joseph and pray to them. The first example is art, the second idolatry.

Another question is whether we are allowed to "play around" with reality in our art. Can I paint a picture of pink cats and purple cabbages? God has answered that question already. In Exodus 28:33, in giving instructions for the high priest's robes, God commands, "Make pomegranates of blue, purple and scarlet yarn around the hem of the robe, with gold bells between them."

Blue pomegranates? In reality, the fruit is reddish-orange. This, I believe, gives people freedom to imaginatively render reality—to transcend the natural. Take, for example, expressionism (an art form in which artists sought to represent feelings and mood rather than objective reality, usually distorting color and form) and impressionism (a style of painting that concentrates on the general impression of a scene without going into great detail). An example of expressionism would be Picasso's *Guernica* or van Gogh's *Starry Night*. An example of impressionism would be Monet's *Water Lilies* or Manet's *On the Beach*.

Compare this, by the way, with Islamic art. Now I love Islamic art—it has great intricacy, balance, symmetry, and sense of color. But let me stress that I love the form, not the content. In fact, Islamic art has no content; it is abstract. Muslims take the commandment against idolatry so seriously that they will never create a work of art that represents anything in the real world, be it a cat or a caliph—and to make an image of Allah or Muhammad is idolatry of the highest order.

Degenerate Art

One reason so many people react negatively to "art" is because there's so much bad art out there. The rise of postmodernism and existentialism, with a healthy dose of nihilism thrown in, stripped Western culture of any concept of absolute truth, and standards for beauty flew out the window with it. If life is meaningless and we have to create our own meaning, as existentialism teaches, then we must create our own standards for art.

And as strange as this might sound, we can draw a straight line from the Enlightenment to this corruption of art. Because the Enlightenment caused a division between facts and values, art was thrown out along with religion. (Isaac Newton called art "ingenious nonsense.") If art is not "true" as science is "true," then it has no utilitarian value. In other words, art has no bearing on how we live our lives in the real world.

Jacques Barzun, in *The Use and Abuse of Art*, wrote, "Thoughtful people in the [1890s] told themselves in all seriousness that they should no longer admire a sunset. It was nothing but the

103

refraction of white light through dust particles in layers of air of variable density."[2]

William Barrett, in his book *Irrational Man*, wrote, "When mankind no longer lives spontaneously turned toward God or the [supernatural] world—when to echo the words of Yeats, the ladder is gone by which we would climb to a higher reality—the artist too must stand face to face with a flat and inexplicable world."[3]

A lot of abstract art follows this idea. Jackson Pollack, whose paintings were created by randomly dripping paint as he stood on a ladder, took the human element out of art by allowing gravity to do all the work.

The Dada movement arose in the early part of the twentieth century. Dadaists were anarchists and nihilists. They created so-called "found art." (Using the word *created* in the same sentence as Dadaism is perhaps the worst oxymoron possible.) Think of those strange exhibits like a random arrangement of bricks or, in one case, a urinal. Not only is there little or no technical skill involved in their making, thus taking the *art* out of art, the content is meaningless—perfect for an existential worldview. Because existentialism has such a bleak view of the world, much of its art is grim and downright grotesque. Consider what recently happened in Budapest, Hungary—in a recently remodeled wing of Budapest's University of the Arts, museum goers believed that the corpse of a man who had hanged himself was a piece of modern art. Not until the "exhibit" started to smell a bit ripe did anyone suspect what really had happened.

In the musical realm, existentialism led to the cynicism of John Cage, who created "music" with no form or order. It was just arbitrary sounds with no rhythm, melody, or harmony. (More on this in the next chapter.) In fact, he had one "song" that consisted of a few minutes of complete silence. A few years ago another musician "composed" a piece of complete silence, and Cage's estate threatened to sue; it seems Cage had copyrighted silence.

The Enlightenment doesn't get sole blame, however. The romantic movement played a large role too. Remember, romanticism was a reaction to the Enlightenment and led William Wordsworth to call art "the science of feeling, . . . an escape from the machine." If art was guided by nothing more than feelings, then there could be no objective standards. This loss of standards leads directly to someone thinking vandalism is art, and it leaves so-called art critics with no tools with which to criticize—hence the reaction to the graffiti-covered subway cars. They literally cannot differentiate between Michelangelo and a guy with a can of spray paint. It leads to "performance artists" like Annie Sprinkle, who smears herself with simulated feces (fudge in reality) to show how society degrades women. Perhaps the most famous piece of performance art was "created" in the 1960s by Yoko Ono, who would go on to marry Beatle John Lennon. Called "Cut Piece," Ono stood on stage and invited audience members to cut away her clothing one piece at a time.

Influenced by the romantic view of art, Western culture took on the idea of the artist as a sort of prophet, a critic of science and bourgeois society, someone in the vanguard of social revolution. For example, folk rocker Ani DiFranco said, "Art—all art—is a form of activism, a force for change."[4] And in 2003, in the buildup to the Iraq war, several poets who had been invited to the White House to celebrate Walt Whitman's legacy instead decided to turn the event into an antiwar poetry slam. (A poetry slam is best described as a poetry rock concert, with "poets" of zero to mediocre talent standing on stage and shouting their poetry at the audience.) First Lady Laura Bush canceled the event rather than have it hijacked.

There is a certain elitism to the modern art world too. The more ordinary people are repulsed by or don't understand a piece of art, the more superior these artists feel. This Marxist mind-set also leads artists to enjoy shocking the bourgeois middle class. So while great art makes you feel humble, bad art makes you feel superior. Suzi Gablik, in *Has Modernism Failed?* argued that by losing its last vestige of belief in spiritual values, art also lost touch with society as a whole. Perfect examples of this are Robert Mapplethorpe's homoerotic photography or Andres Serrano's "Piss Christ," which was simply a photo of a crucifix immersed

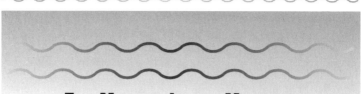

THE MEDIUM IS THE MESSAGE

Have you ever stopped to look at one of the megachurches that have sprung up across the country? A lot of them are either featureless concrete blocks not much different from a Home Depot, or they resemble a shopping mall, with atriums, bookstores, coffee bars, and huge parking lots.

Now think about the Gothic cathedrals of Europe. The architecture of these cathedrals was intended to create an elevated sensory experience; the high vaulted ceilings, stained glass windows, and soaring space evoked a sense of awe in anyone who walked inside. The spire reached toward heaven, and the building itself was built in the shape of a cross. And the craftsmanship was excellent. For example, the Gothic cathedral in Chartres, France, must consist of thousands of tons of stone, yet it looks light and airy enough to float among the clouds. Consider also God's instructions for both the tabernacle and the temple. Artistic excellence was a defining feature.

Now I know God can be worshiped anywhere, and I realize some churches don't have the budget to build a soaring structure. (My church meets in a YMCA.) But what message are we sending to the world when we want our churches to be nonthreatening, to blend in as much as possible with the surroundings? (One famous megachurch won't even put a cross on the outside of the building.)

Some churches scrimp on the building fund, insisting that they can do more good works with the money saved. But consider this story:

> While [Jesus] was in Bethany, reclining at the table in the home of a man known as Simon the Leper, a woman came with an alabaster jar of very expensive perfume, made of pure nard. She broke the jar and poured the perfume on his head.
>
> Some of those present were saying indignantly to one another, "Why this waste of perfume? It could have been sold for more than a year's wages and the money given to the poor." And they rebuked her harshly.
>
> "Leave her alone," said Jesus. "Why are you bothering her? She has done a beautiful thing to me. The poor you will always have with you, and you can help them any time you want. But you will not always have me."
>
> Mark 14:3–7

Are we like those who rebuked this woman because she gave the best she had to worship God? Or are we like the artisans of the Old Testament who used their best materials and greatest talents to make something that glorified God?

in urine. In 1998, when Serrano was speaking to a college audience in Chicago about his pornographic photography, he said, "I don't think that porn is better than art, or art is better than porn; art is just more expensive. The only reason that it is art is that it hangs on a wall."[5] That perfectly sums up the modern art philosophy. (Interestingly, both Mapplethorpe and Serrano are extremely skilled photographers. The problem is not with their form but its content.)

Because a full-blown critique of the arts would be beyond the scope of this book, I highly recommend Gene Veith's *State of the Arts: From Bezalel to Mapplethorpe* (Crossway, 1991). It provides a quick course in art history, art criticism, and encouragement for Christians in the arts.

Precisely because Christianity insists on an objective standard of beauty, much of so-called revolutionary art is expressly anti-Christian, with "Piss Christ" being only one example. (Remember Rule No. 5.) The Brooklyn Museum of Art featured a painting of the Virgin Mary on which elephant dung had been splattered. And Princeton University's Bernstein Gallery recently exhibited the works of Juan Sanchez, who arranged images of naked female torsos over an image of a cross, a ripped image of the Sacred Heart of Jesus, and Roman Catholic devotional items, all linked under the title "Shackles of the AIDS Virus."

Recovery of Art

Remember that anything we create is a form of art. This can be liberating. It sanctifies work. God, the original artist, is described as working in Genesis 2:2. "By the seventh day God had finished the work he had been doing; so on the seventh day he rested from all his work." He called his work "very good." Some think that having to work is a result of the fall, but in fact we were given work to do from the very beginning. "The LORD God took the man and put him in the Garden of Eden to work it and take care of it" (Gen. 2:15). As a result of the fall, work became hard and unpleasant.

But as a redeemed people, work should become pleasurable again, no matter what you do. And we should consider ourselves artists, striving through both form and content to glorify God.

Those who work in the traditionally considered arts must heed the apostle Paul when he speaks of "excellence" in Philippians

4:8. Indeed, the church should be sympathetic to the arts, since both were told they were irrelevant by the rationalistic worldview of the Enlightenment. We must be known primarily as good artists. The content of art will never be communicated if no one wants to see or hear it, and I'm sure in some way it must pain God to have people presenting mediocre work that is supposedly a witness to the surpassing glory of God.

10

Why Should the Devil Have All the Good Music?

I went to high school in the late 1960s and early 1970s, a time when the American musical culture was undergoing great changes. We had not seen such a radical change in musical tastes in so short a period of time as those years between 1963 and 1970. (There was also a great shift of styles within that time.) The lovable Beatles—that was the image they cultivated for a while, at least—gave way to the bad boy Rolling Stones. Pop gave way to psychedelia and then acid rock.

A certain segment of the culture thought the new musical scene was dangerous to the nation and its young people. So someone tried to prove it by way of scientific experiment. He took two nearly identical rubber plants and with the first played nothing but classical music. The other was exposed to a constant dose of acid rock. When I saw a TV news report about this test, they were playing Mozart to the one plant and some really cool sounding rock to the other—Jimi Hendrix's "Purple Haze," to be exact. The rock 'n' roll plant was apparently not doing as well as the other.

So was I convinced of the dangers of rock music? No—quite the opposite. It was the first time I'd ever heard Hendrix (our local AM radio station was pathetic), and I wanted more. I wanted to run to the closest store to buy a Hendrix album. That absurd situation seems a perfect illustration of the fights over music we have to this day. Even Plato worried about the effect of music on the youngsters of his day.

What is it about this art form that causes such great consternation? I think it's because music has the ability, unlike other art forms, to speak directly to our spirit. In the Bible, we see that music calmed Saul's explosive temper. Music is used intentionally to create moods; think of music to dine by or elevator music. You would not expect to hear grinding rock at the dentist's office; it's more likely something soft and soothing. A skillful composer of movie soundtracks can manipulate the audience's emotions in concert with the images on the screen. Think of that screechy violin *reet-reet-reet* music in *Psycho* (the 1960 movie). It perfectly evokes the feeling of sudden terror we saw on the screen.

Back to Basics

Something so powerful is bound to cause disagreement. Should we listen only to Christian music? Is there even such a thing as "Christian music"?

As we did with the arts in the previous chapter, let's step back and set the stage. What is music? It's more than just noise. A jackhammer makes noise, but it is not music. For it to be music, it must have:

- *Melody*: the tune
- *Harmony*: the mathematical relationship between notes that make up a chord

111

- *Rhythm*: the beat
- *Timbre*: the quality of the sound aside from its pitch or volume, e.g., squawking saxophone vs. smooth clarinet
- *Form*: rock 'n' roll, country, jingle, cantata, etc.

You could take that jackhammer, however, and, with a bit of clever writing, turn it into one part of an interesting piece of music. That's precisely what Volkswagen did a few years ago in a TV commercial. They took everyday noises—a boy bouncing a basketball, a jackhammer, the car's windshield wipers—and melded them into a single rhythm that underlay a simple tune. All those "noises," with the work of an adept artist, became music. Or think about the stage performance of STOMP! These men and women take everyday objects like broom handles, pipes, garbage cans, and even their own bodies and create interesting rhythms; the act also has a melody of sorts, as the different size cans and pipes give off different pitches.

Remember from the previous chapter the distinction of form and content. The same idea holds true for music, although not all music has "content." Take instrumental music, for example. By definition, instrumental music features instruments without lyrics. (I use the word *lyrics* deliberately, since some choral music features human voices, but they are not singing words; their voices are but another "instrument" in the piece.) Without content, then, can instrumental music be "Christian"? Patrick Kavanaugh, a music composer and symphony conductor, says no.

> The greatest instrumental masterpieces—whether written by devout masters like Bach or contemporary Christian artists—are masterpieces of *music*. Without texts there is nothing Christian about them that could be detected by anyone unfamiliar with the composers' beliefs or intentions.
> Even biblical titles do not help. If someone listened to an instrumental work without first being told the Christian title, nothing in the music itself would necessarily suggest any particular spirituality.[1]

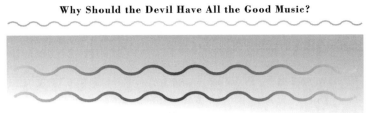

What's It Called?

One difficulty in discussing this topic is what to call different genres of music. Is it "speed metal" or "death metal"? Classical or romantic? Pop or rock? That's why it's important while discussing these issues that everyone understands what the other person is saying.

There is one comical example of avoiding the topic. The Gospel Music Association sponsors the Dove Awards every year, sort of the Christian music version of the Grammys. The awards have different categories: southern gospel, worship music, female vocalist, and so forth. But for some reason they cannot bring themselves to call the category of hard rock what it is. They call it "hard music." To me, "hard music" is playing "Flight of the Bumblebee" on a harp.

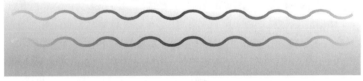

But don't some types of music *sound* Christian? No, not really, except in the sense that we associate certain tunes with the lyrics of a particular hymn. Someone who has never heard the song "Amazing Grace" would never recognize an instrumental version of it as a Christian song. In fact, Kavanaugh writes of a funny incident in which some teens in his son's youth group took the lyrics of "Amazing Grace" and sang them to the tune of the theme song to "Gilligan's Island." With that, the theme to a silly TV show became a Christian song. Amazing, indeed.

113

Are All Forms Neutral?

So we see, there is no particular form of music that is "Christian." But because of associations with certain ideas or lifestyles, are there any forms that are inherently "un-Christian"? Here's where we can get into trouble: Some say that there is no musical form that cannot be redeemed by God, and they're right. In fact, some say Christians should be taking their musical forms into all the world, so to speak, to present listeners with content that they're not used to hearing. The band P.O.D. does that with the world of hard rock, and they do it well.

But is there any genre that is so associated with a non-Christian worldview that trying to put Christian lyrics to it would be like putting a saddle on a cat? Some forms of rap are so connected in people's minds with thugs and drugs and sex that it seems impossible to redeem the category. The same is true with some versions of heavy metal that instantly conjure the satanic images that band members like to cultivate.

There is also the danger of bands trying to fit into this genre being converted to that worldview and not the other way around. But if "Gilligan's Island" can be turned into a hymn of praise to God—well, then, nothing's impossible with God, which is what the Bible says.

So what about listening to "non-Christian" music? Of course, the vast majority of it is perfectly good music—some of it, in fact, quite good music. For some people, this might be a stumbling block. And for me, there are some bands that are so out of bounds, I won't listen to them regardless of how intelligible (or not) their lyrics might be. I don't want to provide money to these bands through the sale of a CD.

In this subject, I'm going to defer to the wisdom of Saint Augustine: "In essentials, unity. In nonessentials, liberty. In all things, grace." This is a good paraphrase of the apostle Paul's teaching in Romans 14. At the same time, I remember what Paul had to say in 1 Corinthians 10:23 "'Everything is permissible'—but not everything is beneficial. 'Everything is permissible'—but not everything is constructive."

The Current Scene

Most people reading this book are probably familiar with the musical genre called contemporary Christian music, or CCM. I like a lot of this music; it's good musically (form), and the lyrics (content) are solid. Unfortunately, I dislike more than I like, which is a shame. Too much of today's CCM is derivative—the "Christian" version of some vacuous bubble blond or nihilistic grunge band. Originality is in short supply. I've spoken to many CCM artists over the years, and some have said they have been forced into a mold that the industry believes listeners want.

Let's look back at the requirements for something to be considered art: proportionality, harmony, simplicity, and complexity. Songs with simplistic (vs. simple) lyrics are set to overblown music, violating proportionality. Too much of it is bland and repetitive, throwing off complexity. And, most important, in a lot of these songs the lyrical content is questionable. No one says a musician needs to be a theologian, but too much of CCM and "worship" music focuses on the individual and not on God: God makes *me* feel this way, God does this for *me*. It's a very American theology, but is it biblical? That's why when it comes to singing Christian music, I much prefer the classic hymns of Isaac Watts, Charles Wesley, and their peers. They combined musical excellence, complexity of harmony and structure, and lyrics that point the singer directly to God—which, for a medium as powerful as music, should be its primary purpose.

And as I write this particular chapter, I'm listening to a CD by a band called Brooklyn Funk Essentials. (I have pretty eclectic tastes in music.) It's a great combination of jazz, funk, bebop, and reggae. The band is incredibly good, with complex rhythms, great musicianship, and tricky, intricate melodies that can only be described as fun. It's this very complexity that makes me enjoy this

115

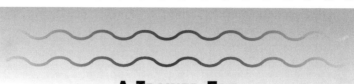

A TRAINED EAR

You don't need to be a trained musician to appreciate music—but it helps. Growing up I really liked the band Chicago: groovy rock, jazzy horns, great rhythms. One song on their second album, "Movin' In," has a curious saxophone solo that, when I first heard it, sounded like the musical equivalent of gibberish—honks and squawks and weird rhythm. But shortly after I bought the album I started to learn the saxophone. Once I became proficient at reading music and playing the horn, as well as familiar with the loose rules of jazz, I heard the solo in an entirely different way. It is actually quite clever, a counterpoint to the background rhythm that still manages to stay within the song's chordal progressions.

I enjoy that song now in a way I never could before. That's why making an effort to listen to music outside your normal likes and dislikes, as well as trying to learn something about it, will yield greater pleasure in listening to all types of music.

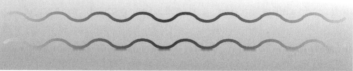

particular CD. It may simply be that I haven't found a CCM band this creative and this good, but I suspect they're not out there. Nor is there a Christian equivalent to Sting or Peter Gabriel. Why? Are no CCM musicians this creative and talented? The talent is there. Are music executives more afraid that they won't recoup their investment—nothing wrong with being a shrewd business-man—or that they'll offend their traditional audience? I hope it's the former, but that itself is a sad commentary on what the CCM market is perceived to be.

A Calling

A final question: must all Christians create "Christian" music? Some seem to think so. William Romanowski writes of several CCM artists:

> The late Keith Green reportedly said, "As for me, I repent of ever having made a record or ever having sung a song unless it's pro-voked people to follow Jesus, to lay down their whole life before him, to give him everything." Can a song really do that, "provoke people to follow Jesus," or is that the work of the Holy Spirit? Likewise, [CCM artist] Carman explains, "I don't just want to spend my time on social commentary because there's too much of it going on and *it doesn't deliver anyone from sin.*" And the members of a Christian rock group said, "Issues are great, but there's no *transforming or cleansing power* in them."[2]

These sentiments are admirable, but I believe they're at least partially mistaken. Why can't one of these artists write a beautiful love song to his wife or a soothing lullaby for a child? Why can't she write a beautiful song whose primary purpose is to praise God, not to convert unbelievers? Why can't he write an instrumental piece for the sheer sake of writing something beautiful? I believe using God-given talents in this way is honoring God just as much, if not more, than producing mediocre Christian music, trying to do with music what is more properly God's job and turning art into a mere tool.

117

11

I'd Like to Thank
the Academy . . .

It's the classic Cinderella story: Rocky, an underdog boxer, gets a long-shot challenge against the world heavyweight champion. Through hard work and perseverance, plus the love of his woman, Rocky fights his way back from almost certain defeat to claim the title.

A great movie, but in the theater where I watched it, it was not just a movie; it was as if you were there in the boxing arena. Men were shouting, people were flinching in their seats at the crushing blows to Rocky's face. One man jumped into the aisle to protest what he thought was a dirty blow. (Okay, it was a theater full of Marines, but that shouldn't make that big a difference.) But there was no real match. Rocky and Apollo Creed never existed. Why the reaction, then?

The power of a well-told story accounts for the audience's actions. As with any good drama, the audience was brought right into the story. They were, in a very real way, in that arena. Good drama has been moving human souls for millennia. The slyly funny plays of Aristophanes from 2,500 years ago still crack me up today. Shakespeare's plays speak so well to the universal human condition that not only are they still performed today, but the basic stories can be pushed and pulled into different shapes and still retain their power. For example, *King Lear* has been turned into Akira Kurosawa's masterpiece about medieval Japan, *Ran*. (*Ran* means "chaos" in Japanese.) *Lear* has also been transferred to the Wild West in *The King of Texas*. *Othello* moved to high school in *O*, and *Romeo and Juliet* moved to the mean streets of New York City in *Westside Story*.

Hollywood has tremendous power. It is the top exporter of the U.S. economy. It influences the way many people see the United States. (No wonder many think we're violent, sex-crazed hedonists.) Hollywood influences the way many people in Western culture see the world.

Take one example: Hollywood's treatment of heroes. Movies throughout the 1940s and 1950s were full of heroes—Flash Gordon, Buck Rogers, Roy Rogers, and many others. But in the early '50s the movie industry introduced something different: the antihero, exemplified by James Dean in *Rebel without a Cause*. The antihero was the central character in the story—the protagonist—but he exemplified traits opposite of those of earlier heroes, not just in Hollywood but in classic literature. He was self-centered, antisocial, self-destructive, and inarticulate (as opposed to being merely quiet, like Gary Cooper's characters in *Sergeant York* and *High Noon*). Another good example is a film called *The Wild One*, in which Marlon Brando played the leader of a rogue motorcycle gang terrorizing a small town. But this movie is an interesting example of how we sometimes can't quite get the basic idea of *hero* out of our heads and hearts. Even though Brando's character is indeed a wild one, he still displays a certain amount of respect, dare I say chivalry, toward the female lead.

But many movies today have lost even that: there are no good guys, only slightly less *bad* guys. A perfect example is Guy Ritchie's *Snatch*, which is peopled by characters so thick-headed you wonder how they got so far in life. (The title *Dumb and Dumber* would have been better, but it was already taken.) There is not a single good guy in that movie. And recently, *The Italian Job* featured crooks turning on each other after a big heist. As a review in the *New York Times* put it, "As is often the case with the caper genre, the criminals are painted as likable rogues whom you're encouraged to champion simply because they're good at what they do."[1] And *The Chronicles of Riddick* actually turned a reformed antihero back into an unreformed antihero because the filmmakers believed that would sell better. (Long story short, the Riddick character seemed to go through a genuine transformation based on the self-sacrifice of another character in the "prequel" movie, *Pitch Black*.) Still, despite being marketed as a bad dude, viewers instinctively rooted for him to do the right thing, which he in fact did. Why? The apostle Paul had a lot to say about this in Romans 2:14–15.

In addition to redefining the culture, Hollywood has the potential to falsify history. (More on that in chapter 14.) Now, I'm not talking about those "what if?" movies that ask what might have happened if . . . There is no intent to deceive in such stories. A perfect example of falsifying history is Oliver Stone's *JFK*, which purports to tell the truth about the assassination of President John F. Kennedy. It is full of paranoid conspiracies, characters who never existed, and dialogue never spoken—presented as fact. When confronted on this, Stone excused it by basically saying, "Hey, it's just a story!" But it was much more than that. I was in a theater shortly after *JFK* was released, waiting for a different movie to start, when I overhead the people in the row behind me talking about *JFK*. "I didn't know anything about the Kennedy assassination until I saw that movie," one said. I had to resist the temptation to turn around and say, "You know even less now."

A Love/Hate Affair

In addition to affecting the surrounding culture, though, the movie business has itself been heavily influenced by the wider culture, particularly by current academic fads. Speaking of this, Chuck Colson of Breakpoint Ministries wrote, "Francis Schaeffer once wrote that philosophy, often dismissed as irrelevant, is, in reality, a powerful engine that drives cultural change. Ivory Tower ideas filter down into popular culture, including films. There they influence millions who often have no notion of what they're consuming along with the car chases, love scenes and popcorn."[2]

So you'd think Christians would be flocking to take advantage of such a powerful medium, right? But you would be wrong. Well, at least until about ten years ago. Unfortunately, because Hollywood started producing salacious movies in the early part of its history, Christians declared the medium off-limits. Rather than jump in to try to redeem it, to take advantage of a new technology as Martin Luther did with the printing press, Christians ran away, abandoning the battlefield.

Even after Hollywood instituted a ratings system in the early 1930s, Christians did not come back. That doesn't mean movies with religious topics did not have success. *Boys' Town, Going My Way, The Song of Bernadette,* and *The Bells of St. Mary's* all did well in the 1930s and '40s. And then there were the "sword and sandals" epics such as *Ben Hur, The Robe, Samson and Delilah,* and *Quo Vadis?* that were also widely popular. Some of these movies were better than others, and some hewed more closely to Christian orthodoxy than others, but at least religion was present on the screen.

That didn't last long, though. With the rise of the '60s counterculture, religion first disappeared, then came back, usually in malevolent form. The hypocritical preacher or psychopathic killer who quotes Bible verses is somewhat of a Hollywood staple now. In the movie *Saved!* the Christians are the bad guys and the few characters who explicitly rejected Christianity are portrayed sympathetically. The problem was that the Christians in the movie were bad caricatures, straw men who were easily knocked down. (More on straw men in chapter 16.)

Today, Christians still are not sure what to make of Hollywood, although most agree that we need to get back into the fray, so to speak. But we tend to talk past each other, not defining our terms.

Should we watch only films made by Christians? Or maybe films about Christians. What about films heavy in Christian imagery or symbols? Peter Fraser and Vernon Edwin Neal say these are the wrong questions. With such thinking, they say, "You are ultimately saying that Christians primarily care about the superficial characteristics of art. We don't care about the artfulness of art, nor its honesty."[3]

As with other arts, Christians sometimes praise a work for its adherence to certain tastes or content without evaluating its artfulness. Fraser and Neal say this is dangerous: "A poor film about gospel truth may be more dangerous than a film that espouses the death of God."[4] That's because people who care about such things will associate the gospel with cheapness, poor artistic vision, and so forth. It will hold no appeal for them. But a well-made film about the death of God may get viewers thinking about the implications for such a world. Well-known evangelist Chuck Swindoll tells of seeing the Clint Eastwood movie *Unforgiven* and leaving the theater in an angry, grim mood. How dare Eastwood make such a movie, he thought. Then his friends reminded him of the title: *Unforgiven.* This is what a world without grace or mercy would look like. Eastwood's incredible talent as both actor and director taught an incredible truth, whether or not he intended to, and because of his name alone, a lot of people got that message.

Compare that to Fraser and Neal's discussion of the movie *The Spitfire Grill*, which tells the story of a woman recently released from prison finding redemption in a small town in Maine:

> Reviews of *The Spitfire Grill* were mostly polarized. On one side were the usual critics who pretty much agreed that the film . . . "slaps, kicks, pinches, and pleads" for tears. On the other hand were Christian critics who . . . thought the film "an excellent choice with several refreshing Christian overtones." The conclusion to draw from this is that Christians who want to see movies about Christianity loved the film, whereas most people who simply wanted to see a good film found it heavy-handed and implausible. That is to say, they thought the film lied. Life isn't this tidy.[5]

Now while this may have been a perfectly fine movie for some, is it an example of *excellence*? Too often Christian movies tend toward the sentimental, which is precisely what makes *Spitfire Grill* a flawed movie. These movies manipulate *feelings*, but they don't engage the mind. Jesus, the master storyteller, could move both the heart and mind in the parables he told. He could take a specific situation—say, a son who squanders his fortune, lives with pigs, and comes home hoping for mercy from his father—and tell it in such a way that a universal lesson was (and still is) imparted.

Another unfortunate tendency is to swoon over movies on which critics force a Christian grid. A perfect example is the Matrix series. Just because Neo was considered a type of messiah, his sidekick was named Trinity, and the safe haven for humans was called Zion, doesn't mean the producers had any particular Christian orthodoxy in mind. In fact, the farther into the series you get, the flakier its "theology" and worldview becomes. Similar things were done to the Star Wars franchise and to Steven Spielberg's *E.T.* But all of these are excellently made films. Although both *E.T.* and *Star Wars* contained ideas that could be applied in understanding Christianity, they were not intended to be Christian films.

But get this: When a movie informed by a genuine Christian worldview came out, it was lambasted by some in the Christian community. I'm speaking of the movie versions of J. R. R. Tolkien's Lord of the Rings trilogy. Some people were hung up on the presence of a "good" wizard. Others thought it was too violent. (It was probably too scary for young children.) Others faulted its "theology." I was a magazine editor at the time *The Fellowship of the Ring* came out, and I ran an article by Kurt Bruner and Jim Ware, who had written *Finding God in the Lord of the Rings*. I got an angry, three-page, single-spaced letter attacking me for featuring an article about such an "un-Christian" movie. The letter writer pointed out how Frodo was a false Christ character because he needed personal works to save himself, how Gandalf the Gray was a subtle trick of Satan to tell people you could have "good" wizards—on and on. This person was looking at the story as pure allegory. He even cited Tolkien to make his point: Tolkien had said of the adventure, "This is not a Christian allegory." Tolkien's emphasis was on *allegory*, but the letter-writer missed the point and emphasized *Christian*.

By the Numbers

Another tendency is to confuse "family-friendly" films with "Christian" films. Some so-called family-friendly movies are either blandly neutral when it comes to faith or actually send a message contrary to faith. Any number of Disney movies would fit the first category; *The Legend of Johnny Lingo*, a G-rated movie about a boy coming of age in Polynesia, is an example of the latter. Most Christian reviewers warned parents about some of the polytheism of the Pacific Islanders, but few noticed the more subtle Mormon theology that suffused the film. (It has been called the mother of all Latter-day Saints films.)

Reviews concentrate on the number of swear words, amount of flesh exposed, and number of drinks consumed or cigarettes smoked, as if such counting is the sole criterion for the worthiness of a movie. I'm not putting down such reviews. Parents find them useful in deciding what movies their kids can see, and I write such reviews myself. But for adults and older teens, should that be the sole criterion? Many great movies would be excluded if so. Other people make a blanket rule never to see an R-rated movie. That's probably a good rule of thumb, but as an overarching rule, it also excludes a lot of excellent cinema.

I was disappointed at the reception *Saving Private Ryan* received in some quarters. Reviewers concentrated mostly on the violence and the language. But the larger message of bravery and self-sacrifice was usually put lower. Personally, I think every person over the age of eighteen should see this movie so he or she can understand the sacrifice our fathers and grandfathers made to ensure our freedom, as well as freedom for Europeans. And for that matter, everyone of this age should see HBO's series *Band of Brothers*, a true story about an American combat unit that fought

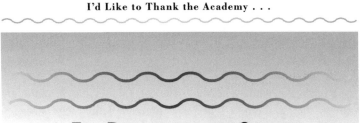

THE PASSION OF THE CHRIST

Academy Award–winner Mel Gibson produced a movie that not only tells a powerful story of faith, but is also made with excellent production values. *The Passion of the Christ* tells the story of the last twelve hours of Christ's life before the crucifixion. With the exception of a few Roman Catholic legends in the story—for example, the story of St. Veronica and the cloth that bore an imprint of Jesus's face—the movie is faithful to the gospel accounts. (I should add, by the way, that those legends, while not found in Scripture, do no violence to Scripture.)

I saw the movie three times, and each time the audience sat in stunned silence for several minutes after the lights came up. It is undeniably a violent film that attempts to show the suffering Christ endured on our behalf.

But as a perfect example of a hang-up with ratings—the film had not yet been rated the first time I saw it in a prescreening—a representative of a major Christian ministry expressed reservations if the movie received an R-rating, since that ministry advised its followers never to see an R-rated movie. Talk about missing the point!

125

its way across Europe, from D-Day to the Battle of the Bulge to Hitler's lair. It's a story of courage, camaraderie, selflessness, loyalty, and dedication.

A Christian movie—no, make that a good movie with an underlying Christian theme—that moves both head and heart is *Tender Mercies*, in which Robert Duvall's subtle performance brings out the hurt of a man running from his past who is offered unexpected mercy. Another profoundly "Christian" movie not recognized as such is *A Simple Plan* with Bill Paxton, Billy Bob Thornton, and Bridget Fonda. This thriller tells the story of two brothers who find an illicit stash of cash—millions of dollars—and what that money does to friendships and a marriage. There's some profanity and a fair amount of violence, some of it gory, but the best line in the movie comes at the end from Thornton's character: "I wish we'd never found that money." What a great echo of 1 Timothy 6:10: "For the love of money is a root of all kinds of evil. Some people, eager for money, have wandered from the faith and pierced themselves with many griefs."

If only we had more movies like these. We should not be afraid to portray sin in its reality and its ultimate consequences. There are many other films, excellently made, that have profound messages but are shunned because of matters such as sex, profanity, or violence.

In Search of Excellence

In the past decade or so, many Christians have come to realize the importance of having an influence in Hollywood. Several production houses have sprouted up to create films known primarily for their excellence before their Christian message. That's the way to be taken seriously in the movie business. Groups such as Act One (www.actoneprogram.com) seek to train Christians to get involved in Hollywood. Their motto: "Act One is a comprehensive training and mentorship center created to form the next generation of Christian artists and professionals. Emphasizing excellence, artistry, professionalism and a personal relationship with Christ, Act One prepares individuals to be apostles through their lives and work in the heart of the entertainment industry." (I'm a graduate of the Act One program.)

Unfortunately, some recent Christian films were notable only for their mediocre or just plain bad moviemaking, *Left Behind* and *Hangman's Curse* being two examples. Many of the problems have to do with money—you can have the greatest idea and the greatest crew to execute it, but if you can't get financing, it'll never get made. I had the privilege of talking to Bob Briner, author of *Roaring Lambs*, shortly before he died. He addressed this issue: "You can get all the money you want to make *Betty Goes to Bible Camp*, but you can't get any to make a Christian movie on par with *Doctor Zhivago*."

Madeleine L'Engle had an interesting insight: "If you are truly and deeply Christian what you write will be profoundly Christian whether or not you mention Jesus, and if you are not profoundly Christian, whatever you write will not be Christian, no matter how many times you mention Jesus."[6]

Compare this in the TV realm with the gay-friendly *Will & Grace*. Homosexual propaganda permeates this show because that's who the writers are; the stories come from the core of their being. Many explicitly Christian films fail because we concentrate on the "macro"— e.g., God loves you—while ignoring the reality of the "micro"—specific people living a specific life in a sin-ravaged world. A friend told me of a church whose only reaction to Gibson's *The Passion* was, "How many people came to Christ after seeing it?" Of course, if anyone came to saving faith as a result of the film, that's wonderful. But once we start judging art for its utilitarian value, it ceases to be art.

Things are beginning to change. We now have Christians who want to use their considerable wealth to have an influence on the culture. They also understand the need for excellence. Who knows? We may soon have a deeply Christian movie that has moviegoers jumping from their seats.

12

What's the Word?

In the beginning was the Word, and the Word was with God, and the Word was God.

John 1:1

"When I use a word," Humpty Dumpty said, in a rather scornful tone, "it means just what I choose it to mean—neither more nor less."

"The question is," said Alice, "whether you can make words mean so many different things."

"The question is," said Humpty Dumpty, "which is to be master—that's all."

Lewis Carroll in *Alice through the Looking Glass*

The cat is under the table.

"We hold these truths to be self-evident, that all men are created equal, that they are endowed by their Creator with certain unalienable Rights, that among these are Life, Liberty, and the Pursuit of Happiness."

Crew tree cats brew kings won't cabbages.

Do all these sentences contain meaning? The first describes an objective reality (assuming it is a true statement)—a mammal called a cat is under a piece of furniture called a table.

The second makes a proposition, asserting something to be true.

The third sentence is seemingly nonsense. Each word in the sentence has a distinct meaning, but the words are put together in a way that makes the sentence meaningless. Ah, but there's your problem: you assume each of those words has a fixed meaning. If you believe they do, then you're a logocentric bigot.

Okay, let's back up. What's all this nonsense about words? Well, my admittedly exaggerated example is used to make a point. If you are able to read and write in a language, you should be able to read words on a page and derive the meaning the writer meant to communicate. But some don't believe that is the case. Let me explain.

A Social Construct

Remember in chapter 3 how I discussed different views of what it means to be human? You wouldn't think that would have much impact on something like reading and writing—but you'd be wrong. The rise of postmodernism, mixed with Freudian and Marxist views of man, has led some to believe that there is no fixed meaning to anything.

Up until now, you've probably believed that an author has a message he intends to communicate, and he uses a text to do so. The words in the text have fixed meaning according to the context the author used at the time the text was written. (This is an important point I'll come back to.) You, the reader, interpret the text in light of the normal rules of grammar and meaning that were in effect at the time of writing, trying to discover the author's goal without superimposing your own biases on the text.

Postmodernists don't believe that is possible. The author, according to them, is influenced by the culture in which he was

129

raised and any biases he may or may not be aware of. He does not stand outside the text; he writes within a certain historical and social context, which is merely part of a larger "metanarrative." The reader must "deconstruct" the text to get beyond the logocentrism—the belief that words have fixed meanings—and expose the sense behind the metanarrative. We can never be sure what the author actually intended to say. The reader, then, becomes the creator of meaning for the text. Authority for the text shifts from the author to the reader. Overlying this is the Freudian view that we must dig into the hidden motives of the author, and a Marxist worldview that sees people not as individuals but as members of a social class and history as nothing but one class trying to oppress other classes.

Sound confusing? Let's look at some examples. Take the example from John 1:1 above. The writer, the apostle John, had a fixed idea in his mind and used words in koine Greek to communicate that meaning. (Translators hew as closely as possible to the intended meaning.) The framers of the U.S. Constitution had distinct ideas about how our country should be governed, and they put those down on paper in eighteenth-century English. The history book you used in school was based on the writings and observations of historians who used various techniques to record events. (More on this in chapter 14.)

The postmodernist would say, however, that John's writing was influenced by his cultural setting. Moreover, if there is no truth, as discussed in chapter 2, then all that's left is power, and therefore we must interpret John's words in light of his attempt to foist Christianity on the world. Similar things could be said about the founding fathers and historians. It is the job of the postmodernist reader to see through these things and to deconstruct the words from the metanarrative behind each of these writings to derive a new meaning for today.

This is the great insight that Lewis Carroll lampooned long before anyone thought of himself as a postmodernist, and he put those words into the mouth of Humpty Dumpty, as quoted at the beginning of the chapter. If there is no fixed truth, all that matters is who's in charge.

It doesn't take a lot of imagination to see where such thinking leads. You have many scholars stating that the Bible doesn't really mean what it says; it's up to us to reinterpret it in light of what we know now. Same with the Constitution: only a postmodernist judge could come up with some of the inventive readings of law we've seen in recent years. And written history is attacked as nothing but a way for the powerful to oppress the weak. This will quickly lead to a crisis in governing and a nation's view of itself—something we see every day.

Gobbledygook

If the postmodern take on writing didn't have potentially dangerous outcomes, it would be almost too funny to accept. But the funniest part is how the postmodernists, who seem completely without humor, don't see how ridiculous all this is. After all, they write their turgid texts using words with fixed meanings to communicate their ideas. I'd love to sit in on one of their lectures and, at the end, ask, "But what does it all *mean*?" If they were true postmodernists, they couldn't answer, meaning they had just wasted everyone's time.

This lack of self-awareness led to a wonderfully ironic academic hoax carried out by Alan Sokal, a theoretical physicist at New York University. He was tired of the nonsense he found on college campuses, so as a joke he wrote an academic paper called "Transgressing the Boundaries: Towards a Transformative Hermeneutic of Quantum Gravity." He submitted it for publication, and the gullible journal *Social Text* published it.

It was complete nonsense from first to last. Sokal first established his postmodernist bona fides by denouncing scientists for continuing to cling to the "dogma imposed by the long post-Enlightenment hegemony over the Western intellectual outlook." He added that science had already demonstrated that physical reality was "at bottom a social and linguistic construct"—in other words, reality is merely one man's *opinion* of how the universe works. And like a true postmodernist, Sokal inevitably brought in the political. He wrote, "The content and methodology of postmodern science thus provide powerful intellectual support for the progressive political project, understood in its broadest sense: the transgressing of boundaries, the breaking down of barriers, the radical democratization of all aspects of social, economic, political and cultural life."[1]

To say the least, the editors of *Social Text* should have been embarrassed, but they were unapologetic, explaining that theirs was primarily a political journal. Scholar Paul Boghossian of New York University, analyzing the incident, wrote, "[T]he conclusion is inescapable that the editors of *Social Text* didn't know what many of the sentences in Sokal's essay actually meant; and that they just didn't care. . . . *Social Text* is a political magazine in a deeper and more radical sense: under appropriate circumstances, it is prepared to let agreement with its ideological orientation trump every other criterion for publication, including something as basic as sheer intelligibility."[2]

The Manipulation of Language

One direct outgrowth of this postmodernist approach is the loss of truth in our language. J. Budziszewski, a professor of philosophy and government at the University of Texas-Austin, writes, "As any sin passes through its stages from temptation, to toleration, to approval, its name is first euphemized, then avoided, then forgotten. A colleague tells me that some of his fellow scholars call child molestation 'intergenerational intimacy': that's euphemism. A good-hearted editor tried to talk me out of using the term 'sodomy': that's avoidance. My students don't know the word 'fornication' at all: that's forgetfulness."[3]

A broader implication of such thinking is the manipulation of language to, in the words of George Orwell, "defend the indefensible." You might be familiar with Orwell through his two best-known works, *1984* and *Animal Farm*. While some think Orwell's major fear was Big Brother from *1984*, in fact it was of the degradation of language for political purposes. For example, in the dystopian society in *1984*, the Ministry of Truth had coined a new language called Newspeak. It consisted of nonsensical expressions such as "war is peace," "freedom is slavery," and "ignorance is strength." A docile population, no longer trained to think critically, merely accepted these self-contradictions as true. In *Animal Farm*, Napoleon the Pig, who leads the revolt against the humans, turns on his followers as all true revolutionaries do. He justifies it by saying, "All animals are equal, but some are more equal than others."

In 1946 Orwell wrote a lesser-known essay called "Politics and the English Language." Here, nearly sixty years later, it rings as true as ever. For example, he wrote, "[The English language] becomes ugly and inaccurate because our thoughts are foolish, but the slovenliness of our language makes it easier for us to have foolish thoughts."[4]

Think of some current debates, particularly those over abortion, euthanasia, and gay rights. Abortion supporters hide behind innocuous-sounding phrases like "pro-choice" to mask the truth of what they advocate. The baby doesn't die; it undergoes "fetal demise." The developing baby is not a baby but "the product of conception."

Orwell anticipated such rhetorical dodges. "In our time, political speech and writing are largely the defense of the indefensible. . . . Thus political language has to consist largely of euphemism, question-begging and sheer cloudy vagueness." He describes this as the inflated style, which in "itself is a kind of euphemism. A mass of . . . words falls upon the facts like soft snow, blurring the outline and covering up all the details. The great enemy of clear language is insincerity. When there is a gap between one's real and one's declared aims, one turns as it were instinctively to long words and exhausted idioms, like a cuttlefish spurting out ink."[5]

That paints a nice word picture of many of the political and social debates we have today. *Euphemism*, which in Greek means "pleasant speech," has been described as a verbal fig leaf. We get that metaphor from Genesis 3, after Adam and Eve disobeyed God and ate the fruit. It says, "Then the eyes of both of them were opened, and they realized they were naked; so they sewed fig leaves together and made coverings for themselves" (Gen. 3:7). When God came looking for them, Adam said, "'I heard you in the garden, and I was afraid because I was naked; so I hid.' And [God] said, 'Who told you that you were naked?'" (Gen. 3:10–11).

That is the critical question. I think people such as pro-abortion advocates instinctively hide behind euphemism the way Adam and Eve hid behind fig leaves. They have a consciousness of guilt even if they cannot articulate it that way (Rule No. 4). Whenever discussing issues such as these, always try to move the discussion to the equivalent question: "Who told you that you were naked?"

As Christians, we recognize that Jesus is the Word, the *Logos* in Greek. He is the governing principle of creation—the *logic* behind it all, if you will. The Word of God, as personified by Jesus and in his words in the Bible, has a fixed meaning. It is not a social construct—not just someone's opinion. Everyone recognizes this at heart—Rule No. 2—but most run away from it—Rule No. 4.

13

"She Blinded Me
with Science"

Singer Thomas Dolby used the expression "she blinded me
with science" in a silly '80s pop tune to describe how a
pretty woman bamboozled him into doing her will. Today,
a lot of people have been bamboozled by the worldview that says
science is the ultimate means of knowing what is true—a worldview
best called "scientism." And while the subject of evolution is the
primary point of debate for many people, something I'll get to later
in this chapter, the worldview of modernist scientific naturalism
that runs throughout much of the scientific community influences
many other areas of life.

For example, a current topic of dispute is the use of frozen
human embryos for deriving stem cells, those little miracle cells
that can be coaxed into becoming any kind of human organ. Stem
cells show great promise in curing many diseases and spinal cord
injuries. There is only one problem: taking the stem cells destroys
the human embryo. Many people, myself included, think that this

destroys a human life, and that allowing this is the start of an inevitable slippery slope to experimenting on humans and raising babies for their "parts." (Never mind the fact that adult tissues such as the placenta and bone marrow are also good sources of stem cells that don't destroy the embryo.)

Interestingly, while much of our culture has been infected with postmodernism, the realm of science is largely untouched; modernism reigns in this corner of the culture. That's not necessarily a good thing, though. While modernism is not necessarily the enemy of faith—many scientists past and present are devout Christians—it can easily head in that direction.

During the Enlightenment, scientists came to scoff at any religious claim. While science had proved X, Y, or Z but was unsure about Q, religionists would claim it a work of God. Modernists mocked this as the "God of the gaps" thinking. God was useful only to explain what we didn't fully understand. With the modernist sense of optimism, they believed we would soon fill those gaps with knowledge, and therefore God would become irrelevant.

Such thinking is easy to find among today's modernists. Some express complete bafflement that most Christians (and many other people) do not believe in Darwinian evolution. After all, science has "proved" it. This arrogance can even be found in the textbooks used in schools today. Modernist thinking is equated with cool rationality while all other worldviews, including religious ones, are therefore irrational. A textbook called *Biology: Discovering Life* has this to say:

> Darwin knew that accepting his theory required believing in philosophical materialism, the conviction that matter is the stuff of all existence and that all mental and spiritual phenomenon are its by-products. . . . And from a strictly scientific point of view rejecting biological evolution is no different from rejecting other natural phenomenon such as electricity and gravity.[1]

Did you get that? If you don't believe in Darwinian evolution, then you don't believe in electricity or gravity, either. This little logic game is a bit of philosophical sleight of hand that I'll discuss in more detail in chapter 16.

A Modern Myth

One of the first things to make clear is that there is no incompatibility between Christianity and science. Christians are not afraid to look in Scripture *and* in the microscope. But in the late nineteenth century, a group of scientists led by Thomas Huxley plotted a deliberate strategy to replace Christianity with scientific naturalism. Several books were published that purported to show Christianity's hostility to science. The books were pure propaganda—the hostility to faith was evident just in the tone of the writing—but the ideas in them gained wide currency, and they are commonly accepted today, even if no one thinks about any alleged "proof" for such claims.

But this idea is exactly backward. Systematic science as we know it today would never have arisen if not for a Christian worldview. Many great civilizations existed before the rise of Christian Europe, and while some, such as the Chinese and Egyptians, developed useful arts that required scientific principles, only Christian Europe developed what became science. Science writer Loren Eiseley says that science needs a "unique soil" to flourish in, and "it is the Christian world which finally gave birth in a clear, articulate fashion to the experimental method of science itself."[2]

Why would this be? Because only the Christian worldview looked at nature as something governed by regular laws, and that was attributed to the fact that we lived in a *created* order. Only an orderly God could create an orderly universe. (Compare that to ancient beliefs in capricious gods who did whatever they wanted.) For example, Copernicus said he wanted to reconcile the many different views of how the universe was put together because the universe was "wrought for us by a supremely good and orderly Creator."

Moreover, Christianity taught that nature is *real*. That might seem pretty obvious, but some worldviews, such as Hinduism, see

137

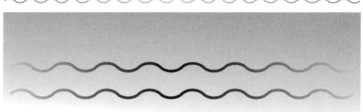

WHAT IS SCIENCE?

Science is a systematic attempt to discover the truth about certain things. A scientist formulates a hypothesis, which is just a tentative explanation for something—an educated guess. He designs an experiment to test that hypothesis. It should be designed so that outside factors that could affect the conclusion of the experiment are minimized. He should record everything to do with the test—not only the results, but everything he did to conduct the test.

This is important, because an experiment should be able to be replicated, that is, someone following the first scientist's method should come up with the same results. If he doesn't, something was wrong with the first test (or the conclusions drawn from it) or with the second test. Either way, it's back to the hypothesis stage.

Finally, a scientific claim must be falsifiable. If I claimed that a magical cat from outer space visited me often, but only when no one was looking, we could never test if the claim is true, because it can't be proven or disproven by someone other than myself.

the world as an illusion. There's no point in studying an illusion. Christianity taught that the creation is *good*. The ancient Greeks, heavily under the influence of Plato, thought of the material world as corrupt and evil; they wanted nothing to do with it. And Christianity teaches that God created nature, but nature is *not God*. Some pagan religions believed gods inhabited every tree, rock, and stream. Such believers would live in awe of nature, but they wouldn't want to investigate too deeply.

Speaking of Copernicus, what about the conflict he had with the established church? And what about Galileo? Wasn't he punished for making a scientific claim that contradicted the Bible? Both men proposed that the earth was not the center of the universe but rather that earth orbited around the sun—the heliocentric theory. This was supposed heresy to the church. But a large part of the problem was that the Roman Catholic Church of the day, heavily influenced by Thomas Aquinas, himself heavily influenced by Aristotle, subscribed to the Ptolemaic system to explain the movement of heavenly bodies. It was a complicated system—crystal spheres around the earth held the stars and planets. But with more observations, it became clear that there had to be more than one sphere. Soon they had spheres upon spheres to explain the different motions of celestial objects. Copernicus challenged *that* view, not the biblical view. The Roman Catholic Church challenged him, not on any heresy, but on the ground of who should be in charge of knowledge—the church or everyman. (Granted, there were some Christians, particularly John Calvin, who objected to the heliocentric theory for religious reasons.)

And the story of Galileo is even stranger. It boiled down to a case of hurt feelings. Galileo also proposed that the earth orbited the sun, and legend is that the church suppressed his findings. Not so. Dr. Owen Gingerich, a professor of astronomy at Harvard, said the alleged conflict was in reality "a turf battle over who had the keys to the truth, one that was especially exacerbated at that time because of the Catholic battle with the Protestants over the way to interpret Scripture."[3] The primary issue was not what orbited what, but "how literally Scripture should be interpreted."

In fact, Pope Urban VII had a keen interest in science, and he authorized Galileo to investigate the different scientific views of the universe. And if that's all Galileo had done, there never would have been a problem. But he presented his findings as a play, with the character representing the pope's view named *Simplicius*. Basically, Galileo was calling the pope a simpleton—not a very smart thing to do at the time. He was put on trial, but he was not convicted of heresy, as the myth has it. He was convicted of insubordination.

And to show that Christians wholeheartedly accepted heliocentrism, it was Johann Kepler who solved a puzzle with the theory. Until that time, everyone assumed the orbits of the planets were perfectly circular, but that didn't correspond with the data. Kepler reasoned that an orderly God would not create such disorder. Under this premise, he kept investigating until he solved the puzzle: the orbits were not circular, but elliptical. Kepler explained, "The chief aim of all investigations of the external world should be to discover the rational order and harmony which has been imposed on it by God."[4]

A New Religion

Scientists today make a lot of claims they are not qualified to make. For example, what should be the nature of religious belief? The late Stephen Jay Gould of Harvard University, a prominent paleontologist and defender of evolution, said it was easy to harmonize evolution and religious belief. All you have to do is put your religion in the little compartment in your life where you care about things such as ethics and the meaning of life, and leave the rest to scientists.[5] Needless to say, Gould did not understand religion, especially Christianity, and he really didn't understand true science either.

And the late astronomer Carl Sagan famously said at the opening of his popular TV series, *Cosmos*, that "the cosmos is all that is, or ever was, or ever will be." Now how did he know that? Had he done an experiment? Was it a logical deduction from a lifetime of study? He went on to claim, "We wish to pursue the truth, no matter where it leads."[6]

Except if it leads to a religious, particularly Christian, explanation. Scientific naturalism is our new god, and scientists are its high priests. As with any false god, it is a jealous god. It tolerates no dissent. The primary battlefield today is over Darwinian evolution.

There are many books out there that do a good job of showing how Darwinian evolution is a seriously flawed theory, particularly those by Philip Johnson, Michael Behe, and William Dembski, so I won't go into great detail here. I do want to show how the scientific establishment seeks to silence critics.

Men like Thomas Huxley in the late nineteenth century to Carl Sagan in the twenty-first century state outright that evolution is no longer a theory; it is fact. Richard Dawkins, a scientist at Oxford University, said, "It is absolutely safe to say that if you meet somebody who claims not to believe in evolution, that person is ignorant, stupid or insane (or wicked, but I'd rather not consider that)."[7] (By the way, if Dawkins was consistent to the worldview of scientific naturalism, the word *wicked* would be meaningless, as I discuss in chapter 6.)

There's one problem, though. They can't explain how life originated. Sure, they say that our planet was once a primordial soup that must have been zapped by lightning, causing some chemicals to come together and—presto!—we have life—or something like that. But the more we learn about the living cell, that explanation becomes less plausible. Fred Hoyle, a British mathematician and former atheist, figured the odds of this happening. There are 2,000 complex enzymes required for a living organism, but not a single one of these could have formed on Earth by random, shuffling processes in even 20 billion years.[8]

The mathematical odds didn't deter Sagan. In *Cosmos*, he stated quite confidently that life arose from chemical reactions in the soup "until one day, quite by accident, a molecule arose that was able to make crude copies of itself."[9] Was he there? Did he conduct an

141

experiment? His chutzpah is breathtaking, but many people accept it as fact simply because an intelligent man said so.

About the only other explanation is spontaneous generation, the theory that nonliving matter is capable of producing life—what seminary professor Del Tackett calls the "hopeful rock" theory. Now there's an insurmountable logical problem with this theory. Science actually proves that life can only arise from other life. How then to explain the origin of life? Some of the explanations are so comical that it is hard to believe that educated people could make them, but it shows the length to which people will hold tenaciously to a worldview despite the evidence. You can file them all under either blind faith or ignoring the evidence. For example:

- "One has only to contemplate the magnitude of this task to concede spontaneous generation of a living organism is *impossible* [my emphasis]. Yet here we are, as a result I believe in spontaneous generation. . . . Time is the hero of the plot. . . . What we regard as impossible on the basis of human experience is meaningless here. Given so much time, the impossible becomes possible."—George Wald[10]

- "Most modern biologists, having reviewed with satisfaction the downfall of the spontaneous generation hypothesis, yet unwilling to accept the alternative belief in special creation, are left with nothing. I think a scientist *has no choice* [my emphasis] but to approach the origin of life through a hypothesis of spontaneous generation."—George Wald[11]

- "Biology is the study of complicated things that give the *appearance* [my emphasis] of having been designed for a purpose."—Richard Dawkins[12]

- "Biologists must constantly keep in mind that what they see was not designed, but rather evolved."—Francis Crick[13]

Crick, by the way, won the Nobel Prize for Science for his co-discovery of the DNA molecule. He realized that spontaneous generation was a dead-end road, so he explained the origin of life

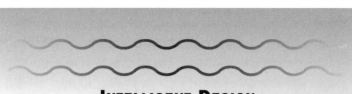

INTELLIGENT DESIGN

The chief challenge to Darwinian evolution today is a theory called Intelligent Design, or ID. Its basic assertion is that what we see in all the various forms of life on the planet and the way they interact with each other could not possibly be a product of random chance, as evolutionary theory would have it. ID got its first big boost with the publication of Michael Behe's book *Darwin's Black Box*. In Darwin's day, the living cell was a "black box." They did not have the equipment to see inside it.

Darwin wrote, "If it could be demonstrated that any complex organ existed which could not possibly have been formed by numerous, successive, slight modifications, my theory would absolutely break down."[14] Behe, a molecular biologist, does just that, pointing out that the living cell is an example of "irreducible complexity"—that is, if a single piece is missing, the thing doesn't work at all. (He uses the example of a mousetrap to illustrate this point.) Irreducible complexity cannot be explained by Darwin's own words.

ID also cited mathematical probability (William Dembski) and simple logic (Philip Johnson) that Darwinian evolution can't be true. Predictably, ID proponents are attacked mercilessly. The chief accusation is that ID is simply rewarmed Christian "creationism." (The two words

Christian and ***creationism*** are automatically assumed to be out of bounds.) Defenders of evolution say it is a debate between science and religion, and they have convinced judges and school boards of this, preventing ID from being taught in schools. But it is really science against science. IDers cite vast amounts of scientific evidence to support their theory, but it has yet to convince anyone who is not willing to be convinced.

on earth with his "Generated Panspermia" theory, which says, basically, that "the first living cell must have been transported to earth by a rocketship on a 10,000 year voyage from some other planet outside our solar system."[15] Got that? It was *aliens*! All he has done is moved the problem back one step: Where did life on that planet originate?

And think about Wald's first statement above. Impossible is impossible. There's no time element to it. It's like one hundred trillion times one hundred trillion times one hundred trillion times zero equals—zero!

The religion of scientific naturalism is being used in other realms, most recently in the debate over global warming. Now I'm willing to be convinced that our planet is getting warmer. We do not yet know whether that is from human activity or a natural event. But some global-warming theorists are not happy with such ambiguity. Stephen Schneider, a climatologist, admitted in an interview with the Discovery Network that scientists sometimes need to goose the evidence to overcome doubts on the part of the great unwashed masses. "Each of us [scientists] has to decide what the right balance is between being effective and being honest," he said.

Be Prepared

Armed with an understanding of how scientific naturalism is as much a religion as Christianity or Judaism, we can effectively ask people who hold this theory for proof of what they assert. Many will have none: they have simply accepted it because that's what they've always been taught.

14

Don't Know Much
about History

A people without a heritage are easily convinced.

Karl Marx

In 1492, Columbus sailed the ocean blue.

On July 4, 1776, our founders signed the Declaration of Independence.

Ronald Reagan was sworn in as the fortieth president of the United States on January 20, 1981.

All these seem to be pretty well-established historical facts. They were recorded in various ways, and historians have chosen them as significant events in history. History is, after all, an investigation of things that actually happened.

But some historians don't believe that is the case. Postmodernist historians believe that what actually happened is no longer important. The so-called story of history is just a social construct, a product of personal interpretation. History can never truly be known because any telling of it is influenced by the social situation of the historian and his personal biases. What's important is what people *thought* happened. And because what people thought happened can change according to who is doing the telling, history can change. As historian Traian Stoianovich writes, "Societies will rethink and rewrite their history as it changes."[1]

Of course, history can be revised when new facts are discovered. For example, for many years people dismissed the historical accuracy of the Bible because there was no evidence that such and such event happened or so and so ever lived. But over the years, historians and archaeologists have uncovered information that led them to revise what we know.

But what Stoianovich is saying sounds like traveling to the past and changing events—like changing the course of the Battle of Waterloo by sabotaging Wellington's plan. That, of course, is impossible and is not what Stoianovich means. He means history is just a story, someone's interpretation. As with postmodernist deconstruction of language, discussed in chapter 12, there is no inherent meaning to anything. The quest for objective historical knowledge is just the arrogance of modernists, these people would say.

Marxist theory has also heavily influenced the study of history. Before, historians focused on influential people and big events that changed the course of history. For Marxists, this is just a bias in favor of the bourgeoisie, the ruling class, in order to rule society. (Remember a tenet of postmodernism: if there is no truth, all that is left is power.) Marxist historians instead proposed "history from below," the study of the proletariat who were oppressed by the powerful. One explanation is that while a historian might have in his possession thousands of "facts," he chooses only some to tell the story and ignores others. Sure, General Robert E. Lee may have commanded the Confederate forces at Gettysburg, but what about

147

Private John Jones in the last rank of the Confederate infantry? Why is Lee any more important than Jones?

Indisputably, historians choose some facts over others, and they presumably have good reasons for doing this. But that's not what postmodernists would say. For them, the choice of what to include and what to exclude is arbitrary. Historian E. H. Carr wrote, "The belief in a hard core of historical facts existing objectively and independently of the interpretation of the historian is a preposterous fallacy."[2] As Carr explains, instead of looking at historical facts as a series of stepping-stones that will lead the historian across the stream, Marxist historians see facts like fish in that stream. "The historian collects them, takes them home, and cooks and serves them in whatever style appeals to him." In other words, the Marxist historian is the *creator* of history.[3]

The Great Fragmentation

A natural result of "history from below" is the discipline of history breaking into many multicultural pieces. That's why any given university has departments for Black History, Women's History, Gay History, and so on. For example, a good Marxist historian would explain women's history as a struggle of an oppressed class against the patriarchal society, much as the proletariat struggles against the bourgeoisie. This is inevitably divisive. Instead of sharing a common history made up of several parts, this view of history tends to pit groups against each other.

It also leads to tampering with history for political purposes. For example, a few years ago the state of New York revised its curriculum guide for eleventh grade history. The new standards for learning about the foundations of the U.S. Constitution included learning about the American colonial experience before the Revolutionary War, the influence of the Enlightenment on the writers of the Constitution, and the Haudenosaunee political system.

In case you've never heard of the Haudenosaunee system, it was a form of government among the Iroquois Indian tribes of the Ohio and Hudson Valleys. Some believe that the founders were more influenced by the Iroquois than by John Locke. There is absolutely no evidence to support this, but for political reasons, it is included in the curriculum. (Some speculate it is because New York has a large population of Iroquois.)

Historian Deborah Lipstadt wrote, "We're in a day and age in which I can make any claim I want. I say that it's my opinion and I have a right to it, and you're supposed to back off."[4]

And the preposterous claims become even more preposterous. For example, Professor Leanard Jeffries, the head of the Afro-American Studies program at New York's City College, has declared that blacks are "sun people" while whites are "ice people." (Jeffries, by the way, is black.) He teaches that all that is warm, communal, and hopeful comes from sun people, while ice people contribute everything that is cold and oppressive. He has absolutely no evidence to support this, but who needs evidence in postmodern history? It fits his political agenda, and that's enough.

There is a large movement that teaches that the ancient Egyptians were actually black Africans and that Aristotle of ancient Greece stole all their great ideas from the Great Library at Alexandria. This theory is taught to inner-city black children to boost their self-esteem; presumably, if they understand that their ancestors were great thinkers and inventors, it will make them feel better about themselves. One problem, though: The library wasn't built until long after Aristotle's death. Again, this fact is irrelevant if it supports a certain political position.

An archaeologist at UCLA has taught that "stone age Europe was the site of a harmonious, peaceful, egalitarian society that worshiped 'The Great Goddess'" until it was overthrown around 4,000 BC by "violent, male-god worshiping, Indo-European invaders on horseback."[5] She has no real evidence to support this, but it fits nicely with feminist thinking.

Oliver Stone's movie *JFK*, as discussed in chapter 11, and the story of Rigoberta Menchu, as discussed in chapter 4, fit postmodernist history perfectly.

The Implications

What does all this mean for Christians? Among all the religions in the world, Judaism and Christianity insist that their Holy Scriptures are based on actual people and actual events. They are not clever stories or myths used to support the power structure. As the apostle Peter wrote, "We did not follow cleverly invented stories when we told you about the power and coming of our Lord Jesus Christ, but we were eyewitnesses of his majesty" (2 Peter 1:16). And Luke, before compiling his gospel (and probably the book of Acts), did some historical investigation:

> Many have undertaken to draw up an account of the things that have been fulfilled among us, just as they were handed down to us by those who from the first were eyewitnesses and servants of the word. Therefore, since I myself have carefully investigated everything from the beginning, it seemed good also to me to write an orderly account for you, most excellent Theophilus, so that you may know the certainty of the things you have been taught.
>
> Luke 1:1–4

If we think these are just facts made up or rearranged to suit some political or religious agenda, then Christianity is without meaning. But we believe that God broke into history in the form of a human being named Jesus, who lived in a certain place during a certain time, who did and said certain things. Most important, he was crucified, died, was buried, and on the third day, according to prophecy, rose again. The apostle Paul wrote, "If there is no resurrection of the dead, then not even Christ has been raised. And if Christ has not been raised, our preaching is useless and so is your faith. More than that, we are then found to be false witnesses about God, for we have testified about God that he raised Christ from the dead. . . . If only for this life we have hope in Christ, we are to be pitied more than all men" (1 Cor. 15:13–15, 19).

And as citizens we should be concerned about the wholesale rewriting of both our history and the principles behind the Constitution. Only a historically ignorant people can be convinced that the Constitution contains the phrase "wall of separation between church and state" and that the founders intended to give women the "right" to kill their unborn children for any reason, or no reason, right up to the very moment of birth. A great deal of political mischief is done and gotten away with because the politicians can rely on the historical ignorance of a large number of people they purport to serve.

If we cannot trust history, we have no heritage, no foundation for believing as we do. It is important to realize this as you make the case for Christ and as you, as a citizen, petition your government regarding certain policies.

15

Curb Your Dogma!

Before she died a few years ago, "Dear Abby" was the family advice maven, dispensing wisdom on any number of subjects. She advised one letter writer to avoid contentious dinner table conversations by never bringing up the subject of religion. Someone wrote in response to that advice, asking if Abby preferred they stick to only bland, meaningless topics. "It is arrogant to tell people there are subjects they may not mention in your presence."

Abby's response: "In my view, the height of arrogance is to attempt to show people the 'errors' in the religion of their choice."

And that perfectly summarizes a growing view about religious truth in our culture. Any and all religious beliefs are welcome. It's merely a personal choice. But if you try to claim that one religion is true and all others are false, you commit the cardinal sin of postmodernism: intolerance. After all, there is no objective truth. You may mix and match your religious beliefs, which is called *syncretism*, or you may believe nothing at all. You may not, however, claim your religion is true. Writer Fredrick Tuner praises syncretism and tolerance, yet he calls evangelical Christianity "junk religion." (He means it in the sense of junk food—something filling and sweet but with no real value.)

So what happened to tolerance? Remember Rule No. 5? *Christianity is dangerous to the world system.* If you mention the name Jesus Christ, the reaction is fierce. The world hates him because his very name convicts them of their sin, even if they cannot fully articulate that.

This seems inconsistent, doesn't it? They are intolerant of Christianity. They would argue, however, that you're too rational. Rationality, in their view, is a Western social construct. And that's the problem with claiming your religion is true. You're relying on objective facts, which assumes we can discover an objective reality to measure our facts against, which is just imposing Western Enlightenment culture on everyone else. Besides, by claiming your religion is true, you devalue the people who believe otherwise. If Hinduism or cabbage worship is right for Sally and John, then it's right. What is true for you isn't necessarily true for others.

A Growing Gulf

To the modern "cultural elite" (politicians, academics, journalists, and Hollywood types), a certain type of religiosity—actually believing what you profess—smacks of the Scopes Trial in 1925, in which a Tennessee schoolteacher was put on trial for teaching evolution. The elitists look at this event as a final deathblow to those silly fundamentalists, who actually believe the Bible to be true and live their lives accordingly. What happened in that Tennessee courtroom, however, was a clash of cultures that reverberates to this day.

Our culture has been moving away from religious belief for at least the last century, but it has rushed headlong in that direction during the past twenty years. In 1992 Harvard professor Stephen Carter published *The Culture of Disbelief,* a book in which he documented how an increasingly large portion of American society has little or no contact with religion of any kind.

But it goes beyond mere ignorance of religion. In these circles, religion has become déclassé—something akin to not knowing which fork to use at a dinner party. About the time Carter was writing his book, political observer George Marsden, in a presidential address at the American Academy of Religion, said, "Outside of divinity schools and institutions with a religious affiliation, voicing a religious perspective is just not intellectually respectable. In

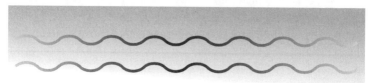

INHERIT THE SHAM

For most people, their only exposure to the so-called Scopes Monkey Trial comes from the movie *Inherit the Wind*. In that version of the story, heroic defense attorney Clarence Darrow confuses and confounds the simpleton Christians, showing their faith to be shallow, incoherent, and intellectually bankrupt. Fundamentalist Christians were made a laughingstock.

Except that's not how it really happened. William Jennings Bryan, for the prosecution, held his own quite well against Darrow's leading questions and sneering tone. He was every bit Darrow's intellectual equal, but that did not conform to the preconceptions of the creators of that film. Hence, today's skewed view of what really happened.[1]

some circles, religiosity constitutes in addition an embarrassing lapse of taste."[2]

There's a lot of condescension in this attitude too. For example, Daniel C. Dennett wrote an essay in *The New York Times* called "The Bright Stuff." In it he described a class of people he called "brights," people who were cool, rational thinkers not given to superstition. They are inquisitive; everyone else is closed-minded. He wrote, "We brights don't believe in ghosts or elves or the Easter Bunny—or God. We disagree about many things, and hold a variety of views about morality, politics and the meaning of life, but we share a disbelief in black magic—and life after death."[3]

Because this cultural elite has so much influence over the direction our culture takes, these attitudes eventually filter down to the "unwashed masses," as some of them no doubt view average people. Because of this, religion is increasingly seen as a strictly private affair. Believe what you want within the walls of your own home, but don't take those beliefs anywhere else. In politics, this attitude has taken our First Amendment freedom *of* religion to mean freedom *from* religion.

Well, not all religion. There's still a type of public religion that's acceptable. It's acceptable precisely because it offends no one. You will hear various politicians talking about their religious beliefs, but with only a few exceptions, none really lives it day to day. A perfect example of this mind-set is found in a speech given by then-governor Mario Cuomo of New York to the 1984 Democratic Convention. It was a masterpiece of doublethink, equivocation, and plain old confusion. For example, Cuomo was very articulate in stating that even though, as a Roman Catholic, he was personally opposed to abortion, he could not force his *personal* religious beliefs on society.

In other words, he professed to believe that abortion was a great evil, but in the next breath said that even with all the power he had as governor of a great state, he would not do anything to curtail that evil. The speech received a rousing ovation, and you'll still hear it cited today as a masterpiece of balancing faith and politics. In reality, however, it's a masterpiece of incoherence.

155

The Death of God

The English writer G. K. Chesterton observed, "When people stop believing in God, they don't believe in nothing. They'll believe in anything." In other words, once you remove any sense of objective truth from religion, people soon fall for anything. That's why we see the rise of New Age religions as well as the growing popularity of Buddhism and Kabbalah, a form of Jewish mysticism based on so-called "secret" knowledge. (Actor Richard Gere pushes Buddhism while pop star Madonna pushes Kabbalah in her children's books.)

What is distressing is how much this postmodernist worldview has permeated the church. Pollster George Barna has documented that even though a large number of people identify themselves as born-again Christians, an equally large percentage of those people say there is no objective truth. A large number also believe one can reach heaven without having to believe in Jesus, that "all religions teach basically the same thing" and "all roads lead to God."

A lot of this can be placed squarely on the biblical illiteracy in the church. Anyone who can reconcile John 14:6, "I am the way and the truth and the life. No one comes to the Father except through me," with "all roads lead to God" is just not thinking clearly. But then, unclear thinking is a hallmark of postmodernism.

Another thing lost in all this is authority in the church. Because postmodernism puts the individual at the center of the universe—remember, self-actualization is the highest good in this worldview—Christians are increasingly flouting biblical teachings on matters such as sex, marriage, and divorce, among other things.

Feelings come to be more important than truth. This is one reason so many people go church shopping. They don't *feel* good about Pastor X or the worship music at Church Y, so they go looking for a better experience. Remember, postmodernists say our experiences and feelings determine truth. I think it accounts for the popularity of so-called "worship" music too. Some of this music is fine, but too much of it depends on repetition and emotions. There is precious little doctrinal truth in a lot of it. It's all about how I *feel* about God. The focus moves from God to the worshiper.

Speaking of doctrine, Christians believe that Jesus died, was buried, and now lives again. This is a statement of objective truth—a *propositional* statement. We can cite certain historical facts, including the reliability of the biblical accounts, to justify this proposition. Compare that to the song that asks, "You ask me how I know he [Jesus] lives/he lives within my heart." Substitute Buddha, Krishna, or Tony the Tiger for Jesus, and the song has the same message. Feelings again, not propositional truth.

Of course, there's nothing wrong with emotion if it is prompted by something true, not just the manipulation of ideas. And it is possible to go too far the other direction, emphasizing head knowledge at the expense of the joy we should have in Christ. God created us as rational beings with emotions. It's not either/or.

We can have no impact on a lost and hurting world if we are just like everyone else. In fact, that's why I think many large mainline churches are losing membership; they try so hard to be like the world that they offer no sanctuary to hurting people. They try so hard to be relevant that they lose all objective truth.

16

~~~~~~~~~~~~~~

Your Slip Is Showing

B y now you see the need for clear thinking when it comes to understanding many of the worldview issues facing Christians today. You don't need multiple college degrees to learn to be a clear thinker. In fact, it's amazing how many "smart" people are capable of believing some really stupid things.

The key is learning to listen or read carefully to recognize some of the logical fallacies you're likely to encounter in discussing worldview issues with others. A fallacy is a slip in logic, a mistake in reasoning. Just as you learn to recognize road signs not just by what they say but by their color and shape, with a little practice you'll learn to recognize logical fallacies not simply by what is said but by their structure and shape.

Here's a quick rundown on some of the more common ones you'll run into.

The *Ad Hominem* Attack

This type of fallacy doesn't address the basic issues or the arguments the other side is making. It simply attacks the opponent personally. In fact, *ad hominem* is Latin for "against the man." This is a common fallacy directed against Christians. Get used to being called all sorts of names and having all sorts of false accusations made against you. It's Rule No. 5, remember?

- What does Mayor Jones know about tax policy? He beats his wife!
- Christians should have no say in public policy. They're all bigots.

There's a variation of the *ad hominem* attack called the *genetic fallacy*. Instead of attacking the person directly, it attacks the source of the argument. For example, "Why don't you be quiet! You're a man and could never understand abortion." Being male or female has nothing to do with the validity of an argument.

Or, "I'll never take medicine for a headache. A lot of bad people take drugs, so I don't want to be like them." Just because bad people abuse (illegal) drugs is no reason to avoid all drugs.

The Red Herring

Legend has it that prisoners escaping from jail would bring a particularly smelly fish with them, usually a herring. Once the bloodhounds had picked up their scent, the prisoner would throw the herring in the opposite direction he was running. The scent of the fish would be stronger than the scent of the man, throwing the dogs off the trail. I don't know if that's completely true, but it does describe the red herring fallacy pretty well. It is throwing something irrelevant into the discussion to throw you off the trail. It's important to realize that this fact could be perfectly true—it's just not pertinent to the issue.

Bob: I think fifteen-year-olds should be allowed to vote.

Sally: That'll never happen. Fifteen-year-olds aren't even allowed to drive!

Bob: Yeah, but I think fifteen-year-olds would make great drivers.

Sally threw in something true but irrelevant, and Bob headed off
on that trail, forgetting that the discussion was not about driving
but voting.

The *Tu Quoque* Fallacy

This basically is the "you too!" argument. (That's what *tu quoque*
means in Latin.) It's dismissing an argument because the person
making it is inconsistent in his beliefs.

• Why shouldn't I have premarital sex? You did when you were
  a teenager.
• Why shouldn't I drive while drunk? Everyone else does.

In the first case, Mom or Dad may be embarrassed by this fact,
but if it was wrong for them, which the teenager is admitting by
throwing it back in their faces, it's wrong for everyone. In the
second case, driving drunk is dangerous—and illegal—no matter
how many other people do it.

The False Appeal Fallacy

This one comes in two variations. The false appeal to authority
and the appeal to the people. The first one is using someone who
is knowledgeable in one field as an authority in another.

• Don't buy this car. Dr. Jones, my dentist, says it's no good.
• There's nothing wrong with brushing my teeth with a sharp stick.
  Principal Skinner at the elementary school says it's okay.

In the first example, Dr. Jones may be a perfectly good dentist, but unless he is also a good car mechanic, or unless he can cite some facts for his opinion, he really is not an authority on what car to buy. The same is true for Principal Skinner; he may know a lot about teaching kids, but he probably is not an expert on dental care.

The appeal to the people is a prime tool of advertisers and others who try to use peer pressure to get you to do something.

- Buy Spiffy brand steel wool! Nine out of ten plumbers use it.
- Buy Nuts & Twigs brand of cereal. People in Europe like it.
- This must be the right tax policy. Sixty percent of people polled said they thought it was.

The first example says nothing about the quality of the product. These plumbers might use it because it's inexpensive or their companies buy it for them. The second example has an additional appeal to snobbery. If the allegedly sophisticated people of Europe like something, it must be good. The third example you'll hear just about every day of the week. Those 60 percent might not understand the issue, or they have selfish motives for believing as they do. It has nothing to do with what is the best policy.

The Straw Man Fallacy

It wouldn't be too hard to win a fight against a straw man, would it? This fallacy happens when someone either exaggerates or misstates your argument to make it easier to beat.

- Christians believe all women should get pregnant, stay home with the children, and never have a job outside the house.
- Dad: I don't think you should be watching this TV show.
  Son: Oh, great. Now you want me to spend the rest of my life in my bedroom!

161

The first example is an obvious overstatement of what some Christians might believe. The second example uses exaggeration to make it sound like Dad's comment is unreasonable.

The False Assumption

An assumption is accepting something as true without proof. Be especially careful of assumptive language. If you buy the assumption (even if you don't realize you're doing so), you buy the argument.

- Since all Christians hate homosexuals, they should not be allowed to vote on this issue.
- Christians tend to be dumb, so they shouldn't be allowed in politics.

These examples don't need explanation, but many people use variations on these arguments.

The Circular Argument

This happens when you say A is true because B is true, and B is true because A is true. It's like a cat chasing its tail.

Bob: Trust me. I'd never lie to you because I'm a Christian.
Sally: How do I know you're a Christian?
Bob: Because I never lie.

Be especially careful not to use circular reasoning when you defend the authority of Scripture. The argument goes like this: You say the Bible is the authoritative Word of God because it says it is the authoritative Word of God. That, of course, is true, but it does not base its claim on circular reason. Numerous times

162

the Bible tells us to look to the evidence to show that the Bible is trustworthy. It is not the Bible verifying itself.

Equivocation

This happens when you're both using a word, but each is using it with a different meaning.

- That dog just escaped from his pen!
  His pen!? I don't see any ink.
- It's bad to drink and drive.
  I'd better not play golf then.

In the first example, the word *pen* means "enclosure" and "writing instrument." In the second example, *drive* means to steer a car and to tee off with a golf ball.

The Loaded Question

Sometimes called begging the question, the loaded question assumes something to be true by including it in the question. The most famous example is "When did you stop beating your wife?" It assumes the man is a wife-beater before asking the question. If he's not a wife-beater, it's an impossible question to answer, because by saying, "I haven't," it's interpreted to mean he hasn't stopped beating his wife, not that he never did so in the first place.

- What did you use to clean up the milk you spilled?
- Do you favor going to war against Iraq if it is the only way to stop terrorists?
- Why do you keep bugging the cat by doing that?

163

The first example assumes you spilled the milk in the first place. The second example is common in political polling. The person is actually being asked two questions; he may favor going to war against Iraq, but not because it's a way to stop terrorists. Or he might favor stopping terrorists but not by going to war against Iraq. The third example assumes that what you're doing bugs the cat.

17

The Primacy of the Gospel

You have now learned a bit about how we got where we are today as a culture and what you can do in response. It can be depressing sometimes, looking at the world around you, but it is important to remember that we have a great hope ahead of us. This may sound trite, but God *is* in control.

I have a final important point to make. Knowledge is power, and you probably have knowledge now that you didn't have before you started this book. If I've communicated only one thing in this book, it's that we are not to do things the way the world does. That said, this power you have should be used *passively*—that is, not as a weapon but as an interpretive tool. Use this tool to analyze what you're hearing and to formulate a response. And here's an important insight: every time the Bible uses the words *grace* and *truth* together, guess which one always comes first. Consider these passages (emphases mine):

- John 1:1: "The Word became flesh and made his dwelling among us. We have seen his glory, the glory of the One and Only, who came from the Father, full of *grace* and *truth*."

- John 1:17: "For the law was given through Moses; *grace* and *truth* came through Jesus Christ."

- Colossians 1:6: "All over the world this gospel is bearing fruit and growing, just as it has been doing among you since the day you heard it and understood God's *grace* in all its *truth*."

- 2 John 1:3: "*Grace*, mercy and peace from God the Father and from Jesus Christ, the Father's Son, will be with us in *truth* and love."

Our primary weapon is one the world would never consider using: grace. No matter how wrong you think someone is, no matter how obnoxious he is in responding to you, always remember this truth. The apostle Paul said it better than I ever could.

> Your attitude should be the same as that of Christ Jesus: Who, being in very nature God, did not consider equality with God something to be grasped, but made himself nothing, taking the very nature of a servant, being made in human likeness. And being found in appearance as a man, he humbled himself and became obedient to death—even death on a cross!
>
> Philippians 2:5–8

Our job is not to win arguments; it's to state and defend the truth. If you take on the attitude that changing minds is your job and your job only, you'll give yourself a lot of heartburn. In the end, it is God who changes hearts and minds. A lot of so-called culture warriors give themselves a lot of heartburn by not remembering this. (Some also give an unbelieving world an opportunity to blaspheme God because of their attitude and words.)

I'm not saying that you should not be involved in the public arena; if anything, I'm encouraging you to do so. It is our responsibility as salt and light, not to mention our right as citizens, to point the way toward a good society, to fight evil, and to promote the public good. But remember who it is who really fights the battle and do not become discouraged if everything seems to go against you.

Our primary duty is to preach the gospel. We can win all the cultural and intellectual arguments, but if we alienate people by our attitude and words, we have lost more than just an argument—we have lost an opportunity to be a good witness. Remember, *grace* and then *truth*.

So I close with the following advice from the apostle Peter:

Always be prepared to give an answer to everyone who asks you to give the reason for the hope that you have. But do this with gentleness and respect, keeping a clear conscience, so that those who speak maliciously against your good behavior in Christ may be ashamed of their slander. It is better, if it is God's will, to suffer for doing good than for doing evil.

1 Peter 3:15–17

Notes

Introduction

1. David S. Dockery, "Toward a Foundational Worldview," The Wilberforce Forum, *Findings* Online Journal 2, no. 1 (Fall 2002), 3. http://www.pfm.org/ Wilberforcetemplate.cfm?Section=Wilberforce_Home&CONTENTID=2886& TEMPLATE=/ContentManagement/ContentDisplay.cfm

Chapter 3: Behold, Man!

1. From a promotional brochure by the American Humanist Association as quoted in Tim LaHaye and David Noebel, *Mind Siege* (Nashville: W. Publishing Group, 2003), 74.

2. Julian Huxley, "The New Divinity," in Chatto & Windus, *Essays of a Humanist*, 1964. http://www.update.uu.se/~fbendz/library/jh_divin.htm

3. Carl Rogers, *Journal of Humanistic Psychology* (Summer 1982): 8.

4. Abraham H. Maslow, *Toward a Psychology of Being* (New York: Wiley, 1998), 5.

Chapter 4: Neither Greek nor Jew . . .

1. Andree Seu, *World* magazine 18, no. 9 (March 8, 2003).

2. Reported in Josh McDowell, *The New Tolerance* (Wheaton: Tyndale, 1998), 43.

3. Ibid., 53–68.

Chapter 5: Do the Right Thing

1. J. P. Moreland and William Lane Craig, *Philosophical Foundations for a Christian Worldview* (Downers Grove, IL: InterVarsity Press, 2003), 394–95.

2. Quoted in Michael Curtis, *The Great Political Theories*, 2 (New York: Avon, 1981), 117.

3. Quoted in Mortimer J. Adler, *How to Think about the Great Ideas: From the Great Books of Western Civilization* (Chicago: Open Court, 2000), 90.

4. John Dewey, *Reconstructions in Philosophy*, quoted in *American Political Science Review* 66, no. 3 (September 1972): 796–817.

5. C. S. Lewis, *The Abolition of Man* (San Francisco: HarperSanFrancisco, 2001), 26.

Chapter 6: Stop in the Name of the Law!

1. Justices Sandra Day O'Connor, Anthony Kennedy, and David Souter in "Planned Parenthood v. Casey (1992)" in *The Abortion Controversy: A Reader*, eds. Louis P. Pojman and Francis Beckwith (Belmont, CA: Wadsworth, 1994), 54.

2. Hadley Arkes, "A Pride of Bootless Friends: Some Melancholy Reflections on the Current State of the Pro-Life Movement," in *Life and Learning IV: Proceedings of the Fourth University Faculty for Life Conference*, ed. Joseph Koterski (Washington DC: University Faculty for Life, 1995), 19.

Chapter 7: You Can't Fight City Hall

1. See Canada's hate-crime legislation at http://laws.justice.gc.ca/en/c-46/41491.html

2. John W. Whitehead, *The Second American Revolution* (Elgin, IL: Cook, 1982), 113.

3. Thomas Jefferson, *Notes on the State of Virginia* (Philadelphia: Matthew Carey, 1794), Query XVIII, 237, quoted in David Barton, "The Separation of Church and State." http://www.wallbuilders.com/resources/search/detail.php?ResourceID=9

Chapter 8: To Have and to Hold

1. Maggie Gallagher, "The Stakes: Why We Need Marriage," *National Review* Online, July 14, 2003. http://www.nationalreview.com/comment/comment-gallagher071403.asp. Gallagher is the coauthor with Linda J. Waite of *The Case for Marriage: Why Married People Are Happier, Healthier, and Better Off Financially* (New York: Doubleday, 2000).

2. Sam Schulman, "Gay Marriage and Marriage," *Commentary* 116, no. 4 (November 2003) http://www.commentarymagazine.com

3. Phil Stringer, "Militant Feminism," http://www.usiap.org/Viewpoints/Family/Unit/MilitantFeminism.html

4. Al and Tipper Gore, *Joined at the Heart: The Transformation of the American Family* (New York: Henry Holt, 2002), 341.

5. Ibid., 57.

6. Gallagher, "The Stakes."

7. Schulman, "Gay Marriage and Marriage."

Chapter 9: Art for Art's Sake

1. Gene Edward Veith, *State of the Arts: From Bezalel to Mapplethorpe* (Wheaton: Crossway, 1991), 47–48.

2. Jacques Barzun, *The Use and Abuse of Art* (Princeton, NJ: Princeton University Press, 1975), 25.

3. William Barrett, *Irrational Man* (Garden City, NY: Doubleday, 1958).

4. Ani DiFranco, *Seventeen*, June 2003.

5. Andres Serrano, http://www.chronicle.com/back/1999_spring/99feb22

Chapter 10: Why Should the Devil Have All the Good Music?

1. Patrick Kavanaugh, *Worship—a Way of Life* (Grand Rapids: Chosen, 2001), 145.

2. William D. Romanowski, *Eyes Wide Open: Looking for God in Popular Culture* (Grand Rapids: Brazos, 2001), 69–70.

Chapter 11: I'd Like to Thank the Academy . . .

1. Stephen Holden, review of *The Italian Job*, *New York Times*, May 30, 2003, late edition, sec. E13.

2. *BreakPoint* with Charles Colson, "Celluloid Philosophy Lessons: What Is Hollywood Teaching Your Teen?" June 25, 2003.

3. Peter Fraser, *ReViewing the Movies* (Wheaton: Crossway, 2000), 32.

4. Ibid., 33.

5. Ibid., 26.

6. Madeleine L'Engle, *Walking on Water: Reflections on Faith and Art* (New York: North Point, 1995), 121–22.

Chapter 12: What's the Word?

1. Alan D. Sokal, *Social Text*, Spring/Summer 1996. http://www.physics.nyu.edu/faculty/sokal/transgress_v2/transgress_v2_singlefile.html

2. Paul A. Boghossian, "What the Sokal Hoax Ought to Teach Us: The Pernicious Consequences and Internal Contradictions of 'Postmodernist' Relativism," Commentary, *Times Literary Supplement*, December 13, 1996, 14–15.

3. J. Budziszewski, *The Revenge of Conscience* (Dallas: Spence, 1999), 21.

4. George Orwell, *A Collection of Essays* (New York: Harcourt, 1979), 156–57.

5. Ibid., 156.

Chapter 13: "She Blinded Me with Science"

1. Joseph S. Levine and Kenneth R. Miller, *Biology: Discovering Life* (Lexington, MA: D.C. Heath, 1994), 161, quoted in Dennis McCallum, ed., *The Death of Truth* (Minneapolis: Bethany, 1996), 180.

2. Loren Eiseley, quoted in Nancy Pearcy and Charles B. Thaxton, *The Soul of Science: Christian Faith and Natural Philosophy* (Wheaton: Crossway, 1994), 17–18.

3. Owen Gingerich, "The Galileo Affair," *Scientific American*, August 1982.

4. Morris Kline, *Mathematics in Western Culture* (New York: Oxford University Press, 1980), 31.

5. Stephen Jay Gould, "Dorothy, It's Really Oz: A Pro-creationist Decision in Kansas Is More than a Blow against Darwin," *Time*, August 23, 1999.

6. Carl Sagan, "The Shores of the Cosmos," episode 1 in *Cosmos* DVD set (Cosmos Studios, 2000).

7. Richard Dawkins, "Ignorance Is No Crime," *Free Inquiry* magazine Vol. 21, no. 3. http://secularhumanism.org/library/fi/dawkins_21_3.html

8. Fred Hoyle's answer to Richard Dawkins's *The Blind Watchmaker* at http://library.thinkquest.org/27407/creation/chances.htm

9. Carl Sagan, *Cosmos* (New York: Ballantine, 1993), 282.

10. George Wald, "The Origin of Life," *Scientific American*, August 1954, 45.

11. Ibid., 47.

12. Richard Dawkins, *The Blind Watchmaker* (New York: Norton, 1996), 1.

13. Francis Crick, *What Mad Pursuit* (New York: Basic Books, 1988), 138.

14. Charles Darwin, *On the Origin of Species* (New York: Gramercy, 1985), 219.

15. F. H. C. Crick and L. E. Orgel, "Directed Panspermia," *Icarus*, Vol. 19 (1973): 341.

Chapter 14: Don't Know Much about History

1. Traian Stoianovich, *French Historical Method: The Annales Paradigm* (Ithaca, NY: Cornell University Press, 1976), 35, quoted in McCallum, *The Death of Truth*.

2. E. H. Carr, *What Is History?* (New York: Random, 1961), 10, quoted in McCallum, *The Death of Truth*.

3. Ibid., 6.

4. Deborah E. Lipstadt, *Denying the Holocaust: The Growing Assault on Truth and Memory* (New York: Free Press, 1993), quoted in McCallum, *The Death of Truth*.

5. Quoted in McCallum, *The Death of Truth*, 139.

Chapter 15: Curb Your Dogma!

1. Carol Iannone, "The Truth about *Inherit the Wind*," *First Things*, 70 (February 1997): 28-33. http://www.firstthings.com/ftissues/ft9702/articles/iannone.html

2. Cullen Murphy, "Religion and the Cultural Elite," *The Atlantic Monthly*, April 7, 1994.

3. Daniel C. Dennett, "The Bright Stuff," The *New York Times*, July 12, 2003, 11.

Tom Neven is senior editor for *Plugged In* magazine and the former editor of *Focus on the Family* magazine. He has written for a variety of publications, including Time-Life, *Writer's Digest*, the *Washington Post*, and the *Denver Post*. He is a graduate of Wheaton College and the Columbia University Graduate School of Journalism.